SPIRITUAL
REGRESSION
for peace & healing

About the Author

Renowned Swiss spiritual regression hypnotherapist Ursula Demarmels (Austria) studied in Switzerland and Germany. She is a Scientific Associate for Research at the University of Salzburg, teaching relaxation and hypnosis methods, and has had a spiritual regression practice for more than thirty years. She has guided some 4,000 people into their past lives and their eternal life as a divine soul in the spirit world. According to some of Europe's largest TV stations, Ursula Dermarmels can be regarded as Europe's most successful expert on spiritual regression hypnotherapy and historically verifiable reincarnation. Through her regression documentary programs, she has already reached more than 47 million TV viewers in the German-speaking countries. Demarmels has dedicated her life to the application of spiritual insights for humanitarian concerns, with the goal of a harmonious co-existence of humans, animals, and nature. Visit her bilingual website at:

www.spiritualregression.de

URSULA DEMARMELS

SPIRITUAL REGRESSION

for peace & healing

discover your life
mission through past
life exploration

Llewellyn Publications
Woodbury, Minnesota

FIRST EDITION
First Printing, 2015

Cover art: iStockphoto.com/16502363/©LPETTET,
          iStockphoto.com/ 37915738/©Roxana_ro
Cover design: Kevin R. Brown
Translation: Adam Gordon

Llewellyn Publications is a registered trademark of Llewellyn Worldwide, Ltd.

Library of Congress Cataloging-in-Publication Data
Demarmels, Ursula.
  Spiritual regression for peace & healing : discover your life mission through past life exploration / by Ursula Demarmels.—First Edition.
     pages cm
  Includes bibliographical references.
  ISBN 978-0-7387-3994-6
  1. Reincarnation. I. Title. II. Title: Spiritual regression for peace and healing.
  BP573.R5D46 2015
  133.901'35—dc23
                          2015012051

Llewellyn Publications
A Division of Llewellyn Worldwide Ltd.
2143 Wooddale Drive
Woodbury, MN 55125-2989
www.llewellyn.com

Printed in the United States of America

Acknowledgments

My deep gratitude goes out to the spirit world, my excellent teachers, my clients, my heart family, and all the other dear beings who, directly or indirectly, have helped this book come to fruition.

I feel myself to be profoundly connected with all the light workers in the human, animal, and plant worlds and in the other worlds and dimensions as well.

In appreciation, gratitude, and joy,

~Ursula Demarmels

Contents

Preface

By Michael Aufhauser

Well into my forties, I had a gnawing desire to do more for humanity, to make a difference and thus give back to this earthly world in some significant way. I saw my friends helping people in their work, which I found admirable. My initial thought was to raise awareness of the plight of the weaker members of society, young and old, the helpless, scared, lonely, and forgotten.

As far back as I could remember, I had a burning love for animals deeply embedded within my soul. When I contemplated the journey forward, I held steadfast to the notion that simple, pure, compassionate living not only aids those who are weak, abused, and dependent, but also beneficially influences all people.

Money, ego, and power are the key motivations in abusive situations against all beings, human and nonhuman. Factory farming, hunting, breeding, animal research, and animal sports are all products of the superiority complex of humans.

My journey began by first giving up my private riding stables. My horses, never to be ridden again, were now allowed to really enjoy their existence on this planet. I named my estate Gut Aiderbichl (www.gut-aiderbichl.com) and opened up my home and stables to over three million people in the last ten years. Today there are twenty-six sanctuaries in four European countries. Our facilities combined create the largest sanctuary organization in all of Europe.

More than 6,000 rescued animals call Gut Aiderbichl their forever home. More than 300 dedicated employees tend to their needs and ensure that no stress or harm will befall them again. From the chimpanzees freed from over thirty years of imprisonment in their tiny laboratory cages to the 700 abused horses and 500 pigs and cattle rescued from slaughterhouses, all of these sentient creatures are protected from harm inside the gates of Gut Aiderbichl. The most famous cow, Yvonne, escaped while being transported to the slaughterhouse. Her fugitive days of hiding and escaping capture made headline news around the world. People everywhere began to embrace and understand the philosophy of Gut Aiderbichl. It is a simple philosophy that awakens our inner peace and reminds us of our values buried so deep within our being that they have begun to fade away.

To more accurately look behind the scenes of our life, a spiritual regression into a previous life can assist us in recognizing the deeper meaning of life and gathering information for our future path or our current life. In 2001 I met Ursula Demarmels and her husband, Professor Dr. Gerhard W. Hacker. Both became members of Gut Aiderbichl and sponsored animals in need. We became great friends over the years. Ursula's success in spiritual regression deeply impressed me. When I personally experienced her unique sessions, it was a very touching experience that connected me with inner peace and tranquility.

Our common goal is the quest for a world in which every living being is treated with respect and has a right to live and enjoy life. I believe that this book will fascinate you, as it is a clear sign of hope for humanity.

~Michael Aufhauser

Foreword

By Michael Newton, PhD

As the founder of the Newton Institute for Life Between Lives Hypnotherapy (TNI), I met Ursula Demarmels several years ago. She was attending one of our training programs in the United States for certification in this highly specialized area of hypnosis. Ursula was already a professional hypnosis practitioner with considerable experience when she registered to study the kind of methodology provided by our program for life between lives (LBL) therapy. This background is what we expect of new applicants because the training is so rigorous. There are numerous schools for traditional hypnosis and some for past-life regressions, but very few in LBL hypnotherapy. Our organization developed the training model that is used exclusively to certify students in LBL work.

Ursula was our first professionally trained LBL hypnotherapist from the German-speaking countries. She has since become widely known in Europe for her writings, documentaries, public appearances, and work in the private practice of bringing a new spiritual consciousness to German-speaking people. We live in troubled times these days in terms of the polarization between religious fundamentalism, spiritual moderation, and atheism. It has been my experience over many years of public appearances that large groups of people of many faiths in all cultures are seeking a new kind of spirituality, one that is more personal to themselves.

LBL practitioners such as Ursula are often called "spiritual regressionists" because regression is a hypnosis term that means taking a subject mentally back in time to their earlier reincarnations. This concerns past-life therapy, but the word "spiritual" also refers to our soul life that spills over into the area of LBL. Much of LBL work involves working with a soul in a current body, that of the client. It is this dualism in our nature that can become so confusing to people in a fully conscious state. The LBL practitioner helps people in a deep hypnotic trance in unraveling this personal mystery. People find greater awareness and meaning in life when they know who they really are and their purpose on Earth. What Ursula and her select group of colleagues are doing is fostering the exposure of an internal form of spirituality within the minds of people who come to them searching for answers about their lives. This internalized cosmic experience is so dynamic that it becomes self-liberating, with the added benefit of learning about their life in the spirit world, which helps dispel a fear of death.

There is a shifting of human consciousness within society in our overpopulated world. This is because of the desire of many people to be set free emotionally from past traditions that have so little relevance and provide so little comfort from the increased pressures of modern society. Learning about our own immortal soul is really a search for self and personal identity transcending our current body. Practicing LBL hypnotherapists like Ursula assist those who have compulsions, addictions, and sadness that control their lives, as well as work with mentally healthy people who are simply looking for personal answers that make sense to them. Spiritual integration brings a serenity within us because it provides a transcendence into wholeness. It is my hope that readers of Ursula's book will see evidence of a new form of self-actualization and healing that they had not considered possible before.

~Michael Newton, PhD

Introduction

For many years I was haunted by the fear that my beloved mother might die. She had suffered from various illnesses from time to time, but fortunately she always recovered. However, my anxiety remained. In those days our neighbors had a cat who became rather attached to me. She was always running away from home and would sometimes wait for hours outside my front door. She would snuggle up against me whenever I was close enough. Back then it didn't suit my lifestyle to keep a pet. I was traveling a lot and couldn't take responsibility for looking after another being. I tried to make the cat aware of this, especially since she already had a lovely home, but eventually she moved in with me. I called her Semiramis and loved her very much. At some point years later, this faithful animal became very sick. I suffered along with her and did all I could to help her. In the end, I couldn't prevent her from dying.

A few months after her passing, Semiramis appeared to me in a vivid dream. She told me she would be reborn, once more as a cat, and I would be able to recognize her by a bloody but harmless injury to her nose, her inflamed eyes, and the very distinctive color of her coat. She would be found in a house with a double set of steps leading up to the front door. Even though this dream gave me a little hope, I wasn't sure what I was supposed to do next. I told my husband and a few friends about it, and we searched in vain for the house with the distinctive front steps. We eventually stopped looking for the house and the cat, and I chalked up the dream to wishful thinking.

Then it all happened just as Semiramis had explained it to me. I was visiting a friend who's a vet and she showed me a litter of adorable kittens that she was going to deliver to a farmer in the countryside. There was one kitten peeking out from under a blanket that I hadn't noticed at first, but when I saw it, I had a flash of recognition. It had a nose smeared with blood and weeping eyes, and its coat was the very distinctive color Semiramis had announced to me in my dream. Was that her? I was doubtful because I hadn't found the staircase from the dream, but I didn't want to completely dismiss the kitten. I went with my friend as she delivered the kittens to the farmer, and what did I discover at the farm? A building with a set of curved double stairs leading up to the front door. I knew right at that moment that Semiramis had found her way back to me through this kitten. The farmer graciously allowed me to keep this special kitten, who I named Lilith and who was a faithful friend and companion to me for fourteen years.

What this cat taught me was there's really no such thing as death, at least not in the sense of dissolving into nothingness, which is what's widely assumed in our culture. She showed me that life goes on past death and that we remain connected beyond our earthly existence with those we love and we can be in contact with them. This also cured me of my anxiety over the future death of my mother, because I knew she would always be a part of my life.

When I had later become deeply involved with spiritual regression, I learned that my spirit guide, who has given me love and support throughout my life, had spoken to me through Semiramis. He was able to use the loving interaction that I already had with animals to make our contact stronger and more intense, in order to accelerate my development.

The Error in Thinking That Existence Comes to an End

Many people are weighed down by a fear of death, either in an obvious or a subtle way. This fear makes life seem limited and often creates a feeling of separation and abandonment. Being regressed into an earlier life is a beneficial way of dealing with and helping to eliminate this fear. It helps us experience firsthand the fact that we have already been here more than once, we have already had the experience of dying, and death does not mean the end of our existence.

Every spiritual regression covers much more than just a past life. I don't just help my client experience dying, which is releasing the physical body in an earlier life, but I also lead them further into the spirit world. It's a way for a human being to learn that they are part of a larger existence.

There is a wide variety of views on life after death and rebirth. The older world religions, such as Hinduism and Buddhism, are based on the idea of reincarnation. In Europe, my television documentaries on historically verifiable reincarnation were watched by more than 47 million viewers. There is considerable interest in these subjects in our modern-day world, as evidenced by the many movies, television shows, and books on these topics.

What to Expect from This Book

In the chapters that follow, I will discuss various facets of spiritual regression. I will shed more light on the concept of reincarnation and familiarize you with the spiritual world and the role of spirit guides in your life. I will examine in detail the actual method of regression into past lives and the spirit world from my perspective as a spiritual regression therapist as well as from the experience of the client.

As amazing as this method for looking into the past might seem, it's hardly surprising that over time spiritual regression has shaken up many outdated worldviews. I have studied past-life regression and discovering life between lives from Dr. Michael Newton, who discovered this way of working. Dr. Newton and his students have regressed thousands of people over recent decades, and clients report that they have seen their true essence as souls, which reveals a sweeping picture of the greater web of meaning in our lives.

I will discuss the path of evolution that souls undertake, the meaning of life, and the significant role that animals play as our fellow living beings in our lives. Difficult questions about illness, sorrow, guilt, and responsibility will also be considered. I will present several edited anonymous cases from my regression practice so you can become more aware of the great potential of this form of regression. I will acquaint you with the broad spectrum of positive changes that people have experienced after one or several sessions. Finally, I will give you a glimpse into the possibilities of spiritual regression in the life between lives.

One reason for diving into your past lives is that it connects you with the world and what is in your heart. At this moment it seems like humanity is in the act of destroying this wondrous planet Earth for the coming generations and for our own future incarnations. In order to preserve our planet, every one of us is called upon to make our own personal contribution to maintain this Earth as a worthwhile home for all its creatures. Michael Aufhauser, an animal rights activist and ambassador for humanity, has created a great symbol of human kindness through his Gut Aiderbichl sanctuaries. With regard to spiritual regression, I call upon all of us to start rethinking with our hearts with the awareness of who we truly are.

As you read this book, I wish you much joy, many "aha" moments, and good things from here on out on the unfolding path you have chosen for your soul and your life as a human being on our beautiful planet. It is my deepest wish that this book will provide a luminous contribution to greater understanding, respect, compassion, peace, love, joy, and connection to all people: to yourself, one another, Earth and all its diverse creatures, your soul, and the spirit world.

chapter one

Rebirth and the Spirit World

Most people ask themselves at some point in their lives whether they have lived before. Perhaps they feel powerfully drawn to a particular period in human history or they have an intense déjà-vu experience when they visit a certain part of the world for the first time. As enlightened and rational as our society may seem, almost all of us still come from a place where we think there might be something beyond our earthly existence. The idea of birth followed by several decades of living and being preoccupied with making everything go as well as possible and then finally death doesn't seem to grant most people any true contentment. There seems to be an absence of a sense of meaning in that type of living. However, this sense of meaning does seem to come into play if we feel as though our earthly existence is embedded in something greater. This divine soul is hard to comprehend but easier to feel. It is present when something happens that fulfills the body, makes it come alive, and binds it into some kind of higher order during, before, and after terrestrial life.

As for me, I no longer ask myself whether we have had previous lives. It's a certainty as far as I am concerned. As a regression expert, I guide people in the process of reliving what they have already gone through in an earlier existence on Earth. For that reason it's essential to assume the existence of a soul. It's clear to everyone that the earthbound physical body dies, but if something lives on beyond that, there has to be a non-earthbound, non-material essence: a soul. It's what will keep on living in a new body in order to have fresh experiences that will help it advance on the long road of evolution.

A regression presupposes a belief in or, at the very least, a hope for the soul's existence and rebirth. Believing is important only as long as a person doesn't know the actual truth. Almost every client I've worked with has been able to get beyond this "just believing" stage after only one regression session. Once this "just believing" thought occurs and subsequent sessions are completed, belief becomes an assumption. This eventually turns into an empirical knowledge based on personal sensation and experience. The end result is the certainty that there isn't just this one single present-day life on Earth, but there have been many more lives in the past and there are more to come.

chapter two

Spirit Guides
and the Spirit World

From the beginning of our soul's existence, each of us is accompanied by a spirit guide. This is often called a guardian angel, a bringer of light, or one's higher or cosmic consciousness, higher self, or spiritual conductor. Most spirit guides have lived on Earth, but have closed down their cycle of reincarnation and have taken on the responsibility of guiding one or several souls on the path of evolution. Spirit guides always steer your soul onto the right path. They give hints and nudges so that the part of your soul that has incarnated as a human being on Earth can progress and integrate all the experiences required for your own personal evolution toward perfection. Your spirit guide's purpose isn't to help you avoid painful experiences, but instead is to help you learn from them. Human beings have their own free will and are responsible for everything they have and haven't done, and that's treated with absolute respect by spiritual teachers.

A spirit guide can appear in many forms, if it chooses to show itself at all. It may appear as male, female, or androgynous. It may appear as a smiling monk, a faerie, a wise sage, or an angel with wings and flowing white robes. It may appear as a dazzling ball of light, an animal, or a colorful field of energy. For some people the spirit guide will continue to change its appearance, and for others it will stay the same. Some people will never be able to see their spirit guide, but they will feel a presence and still enjoy its unique and loving energy.

A spirit guide can also appear as something specific to send a message. One client of mine experienced a previous life in a session and gained some important insights that helped him in his present-day life. His spirit guide appeared to him as a dragon after he experienced a death in a previous life. Because of the dragon's symbolism, my client realized he had spent a large number of lives in China and had a strong connection to Chinese culture. His spirit guide reminded him of this by appearing as a dragon. China played no part at all in the client's current life, but he was now able to incorporate and use some aspects of its philosophy and culture in his daily life to further his soul awareness.

chapter three

Processing Experiences

When the physical body that has lived an earthly life has died, the soul will travel to the spirit world, where it will be greeted by its spirit guide and the souls of others who have left their physical bodies behind. The soul will process its life that has just ended while it is in the spirit world. The soul and the spirit guide will review what did and did not go so well, what can be learned from that life, and what has to be learned or adjusted in the next one.

In those moments when we forget we have a soul or are part of a soul and we lay aside our kind, joyful, and loving qualities, our spirit guide will make every effort to lead us gently back and remind us again of our true being. While the soul is incarnated on Earth, it rarely has a direct conversation with its spirit guide, so we receive messages from our guides in countless ways. We may receive hints in a dream or get to know a person who teaches us a particular lesson. Perhaps we hear part of a sentence in a conversation that gives us the exact information we need or we read something specific in a book that can help us in some way. If you open your eyes and keep an ear out for these signs, it can be very rewarding. Our spirit guides help us get back into contact with our souls.

Paying attention to signs from your spirit guide can be compared with what many people call "listening to your inner voice" or "following a gut feeling." Many voices can catch a person's ear, and some of these can be destructive. You will be able to recognize your spirit guide because it speaks in a friendly and constructive way. The advice you get will always have something comforting, supportive, and life-affirming about it, and it will always be focused on the greater good of all concerned. It always speaks in a constructive and loving way, even if it can sometimes be more intense and direct than normal. If some inner voice instills anxiety, incites evil or threatens you, or makes you feel tired, confused, or disheartened, it is not your spirit guide's voice.

A client lost his mother at a very early age and carried a lot of unprocessed anger inside him. He was told about his guardian angel when he was a child, but he felt it had utterly forsaken him. This man, now sixty years old, lay in a trance before me. I had guided him into the spirit world, but he could not find his spirit guide. His childhood feeling that the spirit guide had never really cared about him started to increase and make him angry. I was surprised, because it is uncommon for a spirit guide not to greet a recently deceased person and make the person feel welcome. I asked the man to thoroughly look all around. He finally found his spirit guide, which was standing to the side and appeared to be waiting for him. The man was gearing up to get angry all over again, but then realized the initiative for contact would have to come from him. When the man then approached his spirit guide, he felt its love and knew that this divine helper had always been there for him. It was he who had rejected the guide and turned down the help being offered, but the spirit guide had never left him and had waited patiently for him. The man was embraced by his spirit guide, and his anger and despair almost visibly departed. He also learned in that moment that it was his mother's life plan to die so early, and it was his plan to live with it and learn how to cope.

Less mature souls will get more guidance from a spirit guide than those who have already collected a great deal of experience on Earth. As the soul's maturity increases, it knows what to do on its own accord. After a considerable number of lives, souls become more aware of their purpose on Earth and how they can best get along. More experienced souls tend to go on their way, for the most part, in a relatively purposeful pattern.

When there is so much divine and loving guidance available, you might wonder why there are so many people who can't get a grip on their lives. People who apparently turn their own lives or the lives of others into a kind of hell don't achieve this overnight. These people have made decisions that have turned out badly. They might not have paid attention to the signs around them for quite a while. For example, they haven't listened to people who have told them in a well-meaning way to drink less alcohol, or they don't want to hear that they have been behaving inconsiderately toward other people. They often lash out when help or advice is offered and feel under attack or uncomfortable when a deficiency or some inner wound is pointed out. They must at some point bear the unpleasant consequences of their own actions or inaction. This can happen during this lifetime or perhaps not until one of the next lives.

The soul, spirit guide, and spirit world are always there, but it's up to us to pause, calm ourselves, and restore the connection with them. It is up to us to decide whether to accept our higher realizations and incorporate them into our daily lives.

chapter four

Spiritual Regression

Knowledge of the soul, spirit guide, and spirit world is usually not accessible to our everyday awareness. However, regression into an earlier life and into the life between lives gives us direct access to this rich treasure. Even after all these years of working with spiritual regressions, it's still fascinating for me to experience how every human being is genuinely rooted deeply in the beauty and clarity of the world of souls. Even if they were very much a skeptic beforehand, those who have experienced a regression are deeply touched and feel enormously enriched. They realize their life on Earth is a great gift and a huge opportunity and feel prepared to take responsibility for it. In the following pages we will learn more about the details of this technique for spiritual regression.

Dr. Michael Newton:
Pioneer of Spiritual Regression

When Dr. Michael Newton started his career as a hypnotherapist, he refused requests for regression into earlier lives because he considered such experiments irresponsible. He adhered to a strictly scientific practice. By chance he stumbled across a client's past life during a session. The man was complaining of a severe pain that couldn't be explained by conventional medicine and sought hypnotherapy in hope of finding the source of the pain. While in a trance, the client suddenly described how, as a soldier in World War II, he had been killed by a bayonet. The client's pain disappeared completely after the session, which prompted Dr. Newton to begin extensive experiments into past lives.

Dr. Newton soon discovered that people are led back to their life between lives as well as their past lives on Earth. This was an incredible discovery that came as a blessing for thousands of people. With every case that followed over the decades, Dr. Newton put together a consistent and useful model of the spirit world. His findings are explained in detail in his books *Journey of Souls*, *Destiny of Souls*, and *Life Between Lives*.

Dr. Newton paints a picture of the different spheres for our souls that incarnate to learn and collect individual experiences in this world and thus bring in more of their Soul Awareness. It was fascinating for him to observe his clients statements regarding the time when the souls were in the spirit world strongly resembled each other. His clients answered his questions about the spirit world with a striking conformity regardless of their religious, social, or cultural background. Newton soon had to acknowledge that he was on the trail of a far-reaching truth about the spirit world that would shake our western outlook and our contemporary way of thinking.

Dr. Newton called his work "Spiritual Reincarnation Therapy into the Life Between Lives." This specific work describes a hypnosis therapy that he has used to direct attention to life after death and to human beings in their soul state. It was important for him to lead his clients into spheres beyond the terrestrial. Dr. Newton helped them experience what happened after dying.

Dr. Newton is often asked questions such as these: What remains when the body is no more? Where do we go? What is the afterlife? What sort of levels and areas does it contain? Who comes to meet us at the gates of this other world? What are we meant to do there? Who is there with us? Why do we come back to this world?

We will tackle some of these questions, though this book focuses primarily on regression into past lives. We owe our knowledge of these fundamental topics for the most part to Dr. Newton and his regression method. I am indebted to him for uncovering a major aspect of our mission here on Earth: we are here to learn and recognize that our separation from our true homeland—the spirit world—is an illusion, and thus to overcome it.

My Work as a Regression Therapist

The fact that a person can visit a previous life with relatively little effort has always fascinated me. However, my initial personal experiences in this field were not very impressive. The therapists I visited stopped our sessions at the point of the death of the person in my previous life. I experienced the process of dying many times and felt alone with all the experiences I'd had in my past lives. I wasn't able to process them properly and became increasingly preoccupied with the question of the deeper meaning of the whole of existence.

Then I discovered Dr. Newton's books. I was fascinated and deeply touched by what I read. It was as if someone had spoken aloud everything that I had already suspected existed somewhere deep inside me. I knew that this was what I had been searching for all this time. A great desire arose in me to learn how to conduct regressions into the life between lives (LBL) for myself.

Now at that point Dr. Newton was an older man, who by then was only barely practicing. I did everything I could to find out even more about his work. I was able to meet one of his associates while she was conducting some LBL regressions on a tour of Europe. She quickly realized I was a person who could offer Dr. Newton's method here in Europe and could raise its profile. I found myself in the extremely fortunate position of being trained by Dr. Newton and his team in the United States.

In order to be authentic to myself and be able to carry out this work to the best of my abilities, I have blended my own knowledge, experience, and skills with his technique wherever it seems to be appropriate and important. Dr. Newton has always encouraged his students not just to copy his system but to "fill it up with your own personality and develop it even further," which speaks volumes about his wisdom and insight.

Dr. Newton's work has touched me more than I can say. Spiritual regression has enriched my life immensely and has changed it a great deal, and I am so grateful to be able to see such great progress and success in my client's lives. I feel that this is what I have come to Earth to do: to help people find their own individual meaning in life and experience even more joie de vivre.

chapter five

The Method

Different regression therapists work in different ways. What they all have in common is they put their clients in a trance and conduct a consciousness journey back into an earlier existence. Most regression therapists stop right before or immediately after death in the past life. They don't work with the concept of a spirit guide, and there's no looking back to see what the soul has experienced. At best there is a conversation with the therapist, who can then express his or her own view, but only from a subjective viewpoint. I am tremendously grateful that I was able to learn this technique from Dr. Newton. I feel it is important that clients can keep going ever deeper into the spirit world, experience themselves as an immortal soul in joy and bliss, and reflect upon their past lives in the company of their spirit guide.

A client of mine had suffered from extreme insomnia for a number of years. He came to me because he had a very strong fear of death, which he knew was the source of his insomnia. As soon as he lay down and closed his eyes, he thought about the fact that he was inevitably going to die. His anxiety disappeared after one single spiritual regression session. His insomnia stopped after he found out about his death in a past life and saw his afterlife as a joyful soul in the spirit world.

I generally leave it up to the spirit world to choose the appropriate past life for the client during a regression. I don't look specifically for a pleasant life or one that pertains to a particular theme, such as one that relates to the headaches that might be plaguing the client. I place all my trust in the client's spirit guide and know the guide will choose exactly what is important and helpful for the person right here and now. Maybe it will have absolutely nothing to do with the headaches, but whatever is seen and experienced may stop them. I can testify that throughout all the many sessions that I have conducted as a regression therapist, whatever life the spirit guide has chosen has always been the most suitable and the best for the client.

With every regression I go a bit further into the spirit world with the client straight after their death experience in the past life. I let them make contact with their spirit guide so they can review and discuss this past life with their guide from a higher perspective. Questions will arise, such as these: What have I learned and what haven't I learned? What have I done well and what have I done less well? Have I discovered my life tasks? Have I achieved them or have I at least worked on them? What is the context for this life? Why did this particular life appear? What is it telling me for my life today? These questions will be clarified in conversation with the spirit guide.

Sometimes the client will recognize people in a past life who also play a role in their current life. The client often will only become aware of this while they are experiencing the events as a soul during the review. The spirit guide can be very helpful at this point because it can confirm or deny the recognition of that other person and even set up a meeting with a particular soul in the spirit world.

I wanted to discuss a past life with a client, but she went immediately after death to a place of recuperation in the spirit world. I thought, "What's this? Recovery straight away? We haven't even done anything yet!" However, she felt so torn up and depressed that she needed healing before anything else. She had to regain the feeling of being a whole, complete being and soul. Once she was able to feel that, she had the strength to look back at the relevant past life. She was in a concentration camp, but she was on the other side: she was a guard. She was responsible for the deaths of many people and was later killed after being torn to pieces by a grenade. These horrible experiences had cost her soul a great deal, and her spirit guide knew that a place of recovery and healing was necessary before she could encounter and deal with a past life and a part of her soul that needed to be healed.

chapter six

Finding Peace and Healing

The progression doesn't always go in a straight line from one stage to the next during a session. Every person and every regression is different. Sometimes clients have exhausted themselves so thoroughly in a past life or have gone through something so bad that they initially go to a place of recovery in the spirit world. In this case, the soul needs to rest, be purified, and experience healing before it can risk even having the review. Some souls will be picked up immediately by the recently deceased or even by friends or relatives who are still alive on Earth as soon as they enter the spirit world. The reason others who are still alive may welcome them to the spirit world is because a part of every soul will always stay in the spirit world and linear time doesn't exist there in the way that we know it on Earth.

My Clients and Their Expectations

People from a variety of professions, all walks of life, and different belief systems have come to me for a regression session. A Catholic priest even came to me for a session, although it was under the cover of absolute secrecy. My clients aren't people you can describe as the typical esoteric types who have already tried everything under the sun and now at last have also come along for a regression. About three-quarters of the people who come to me for a regression are women. I recently regressed a man as part of a documentary about my work as a past-life expert. After the program aired, more men than ever suddenly came forward for a session.

My clients are mostly middle-aged, and I only work with adults. Children are usually much more strongly connected to the spirit world than adults, and I don't believe they need help in connecting with their past lives or life between lives. They have just come to Earth, and it's usually not an issue for them to come to grips with earlier lives.

I am always surprised at how honest of an endeavor this is for my clients. Their inner maturity wants to be uncovered and lived out. They often have not been thoroughly involved in all things spiritual up to that point, nor have they already read dozens of books on reincarnation. Many have no real concept of what is going to happen to them in a session. Perhaps they have read an article or seen a television program about regression or know someone who has gone through a regression and then raved about it, and now they want to try it as well. There are people who have a dream that makes a powerful impression on them and gives them the feeling that it's a snippet from a previous life. Sometimes it does turn out to be true.

It does not matter whether someone has some rudimentary knowledge of past-life regression or not. Once I have started working with a person, I can pick up on how important and relevant the regression process is for them, and how useful it will be to where they are now in their current life.

One client of mine, a giant of a man, complained about how he was treated as the office idiot at work. He suspected that he had been an oppressed woman in a past life. He himself had never done a regression and didn't know much about the process. During the session, he first experienced a past life as a woman who was harassed and who passively let bad things happen to her. The client was not surprised by this and felt it explained the suffering he was experiencing in his current life. As the session continued, the client also visited a past life several centuries earlier in which he was a military commander who was boastful in regard to his own strength and power. The client enjoyed the feeling of all that strength, especially after he saw how meek and passive he had been in a more recent life. After the session, he was a different man, full of confidence and strength. He laughed as he said that his coworkers would have to get used to a brand-new colleague on Monday.

Why Take Part in a Regression?

The reasons my clients come to me for a regression vary, as do their expectations of what they will get out of the session. Many just want to know whether they have lived before and are curious about whether past lives really do exist. They have a sense that more has to exist than what they can grasp with their five senses.

Many people come to me because they have problems with death and are suffering from a fear of dying and the uncertainty about whether there is anything that comes after it. They also want to know what this might be like. They sense that it would be a great comfort if they could experience the reality that they have died before and that everything does not come to an end with death.

For many it's about their relationship with a loved one who is already dead. They wonder, how are they now? Will I see them again in a later life or in heaven?

Others decide to go for a regression because they want to find out more about their spirituality. Many people today are spiritual but not religious. They left the church because they couldn't find what they were looking for there. What's on offer from the present-day religions doesn't work for them and there are too many unanswered questions. These same people still pray, strive to be good, and are sincerely looking for something greater, for a mystical experience through which they can grow.

Many people want to uncover a talent that they suspect is still lying dormant within. They feel that if they experience a past life, they will be able to discover a great talent within themselves. Or they want to know if their partner is really the right one and if they've experienced past lives together. Others wonder if they are following the right career and hope that a regression will help them realize their true career path in this life.

There are also people who come to me because of an illness for which there is no apparent medical cause or no cure. There have been sessions where symptoms really do disappear when the root cause of the illness has been identified. However, this hope is often thwarted when there is no miracle cure at the end of a session. But instead a person might perhaps understand the deeper meaning of their illness through the regression and learn to accept their affliction. Sometimes people come for a completely different reason that isn't related to a physical ailment, don't think about their symptoms at all, and later report back to me, full of excitement, that their illness has suddenly gone away.

Recently I had a very touching case with a young man dealing with cancer, who had a wife and three children. He told me that his doctors had said he would probably die very soon. The regression was his last hope for staying alive. Through the regression, he recognized that clinging to life might not be the point for him and his family, but rather he should let go and trust in divine love and the greater scheme of things. He realized that he and his loved ones would remain connected with one another beyond death. There was nothing separating their souls, which comforted him a great deal and allowed him to make peace with his destiny.

Couples who are in a happy and loving relationship sometimes come to me for a regression in hope that they will discover they were inseparable at a much earlier stage in their souls' lives. Quite often there are connections in which one person has been closely connected with someone in a past life with whom they are in a close relationship in this life. Often their genders and roles are altered. Perhaps the male partner back then is the now a grandson or a school friend from childhood. You may find out that someone you are involved in a dispute with today is the person who was your great love in the past. It can also happen that a person may realize they have treated a loved one badly or vice versa in an earlier life. Sometimes there is nothing there to find of a romance or a beautiful love that has remained from a past life and been brought into this one. It can be a disappointing and painful thing to go through, but is ultimately very educational for one's personal development.

Searching for the Meaning of Life

Many clients seek me out because they wish to come into clearer contact with their inner voice. They might say, "I had so many dreams, ideals, and visions when I was younger. I knew then what I was living for, what I wanted for myself, and what I was striving for. I had confidence and strength. That has completely disappeared over time. I feel tired, weary, and stuck in the everyday routine. But this can't be all there is to life!" These people are ready to take a big leap forward in personal development and come to grips with their personality on a conscious and critical level.

The desire to find out more about themselves and evolve further is what always lies behind a person's impulse to come to me for a regression. The search for a deeper aspect of their lives comes through strong and clear with about 80 percent of my clients. Everyone probably wants to know whether they are on the right path. Some think they have found the meaning of life, but they are not completely sure. Many want help with an important decision. Whether the questions are clearly formulated or are still knocking cautiously on the door of their awareness, there are always answers to be found in a spiritual regression that can help people advance, either with smaller steps or with larger strides.

There are some people who have the hope that they were someone quite special, whether it's a great historical figure or someone who's attractive or rich. In most cases, this expectation is not met, which is how a client can learn to recognize and appreciate the individual path of evolution followed by their own unique being.

For many people, their anticipation can be clouded by the fear that absolutely nothing will reveal itself in the session. In that respect I can put their minds at ease: regression works for almost all of my clients.

chapter seven

Preparation for a Regression

It's very important to prepare yourself for a regression session so you can get the most out of it. It also helps so the therapist can offer what is suitable for the client. At the very first contact, the client will tell me their reasons for the visit, which will give me an idea of what questions I need to ask to make sure everything is clear to them and to know what their expectations are.

There are certain criteria that need to be clarified for the safety of the potential client. These relate to drug addiction, misuse of alcohol, serious mental or physical impairments, and medications. Sometimes I have to turn someone down for a regression. If they are on a psychotropic drug, I will not perform a regression session because they may see and experience something that is not part of their past lives. I will not perform regression sessions on people who are high or drunk, nor will I conduct a session with someone who has a history of cerebral hemorrhage because I don't want to endanger their physical or mental health.

Before I perform a regression with a new client, I send them some paperwork that details exactly what will happen during the session. I also talk about regressing into the life between lives. Many people are interested in this, but they must be regressed into their past lives before they can explore the life between lives. This is very important because the client needs to be firmly anchored in their earthly existence.

Throughout the initial regression process, the client will discover that life on Earth does have meaning, that we are all here of our own free will and can learn to make our lives joyful. Quite a few people don't feel at home on the earthly plane and would quite like to depart from it, so they must learn to love and appreciate their life before they can explore further. The life between lives in the spirit world is so beautiful and joyful that many don't want to leave once they are there. You can use the impressions you receive from your life in the spiritual world as a way of enriching your current life on Earth and not misuse them as a means of escape into higher realms.

The actual day of the session begins with a long initial conversation in which I explain how the regression will unfold and answer any final questions. Right from the start I make it clear to my client that what happens here is primarily a spiritual and not a secular task. In this kind of regression where clients work with their spirit guide, experience themselves again as a soul, and get a glimpse into the spirit world, it's important that they let themselves move into this higher dimension. In doing so, it really doesn't matter whether the client is an atheist or is someone who up until now only mocked and laughed at these things. They will ultimately know better once they go into a trance and meet their spirit guide.

Trance and Hypnosis in a Regression

Many people are afraid of everything to do with the term "hypnosis." They are familiar with stage hypnosis and think I might have them stand on one leg and crow like a cockerel. That is not the case at all with spiritual past-life regression.

Hypnosis is a word to describe the method that takes a person into a hypnotic trance. Everyone goes into trance states many times in daily life too. These states are important because they allow us to process impressions, which is similar to our nightly dreams, but they are also important for our ability to concentrate. During a regression, the therapist guides the client through targeted visualizations and suggestions to arrive at a relaxed state of consciousness. Then the client has access to information from the deepest layers of their unconscious, which they can't reach in their daily awareness.

What happens during a regression into a past life can be compared to what happens when you are asked a question about where you went on vacation twelve years ago. It's likely that you won't come up with anything initially. If you relax and let your mind drift, it might suddenly occur to you that "yes, we were in Sardinia then, and I ate the best pizza of my life!" When you are able to get back into that time frame and mindset, you are able to remember this detail and that all over again. Gradually the whole excerpt from your life, along with the internal images and feelings that were associated with that time, comes together like it was yesterday, even though you always know you are in the present and are recalling events that took place twelve years ago. The only difference with a regression is that timewise it goes a lot further back.

Many people are afraid that they will not be in control during a hypnotic trance. Fear of what will be said or will come through during a regression prevents many from participating in a session. You don't have to worry, because you are fully conscious and completely in control during a regression. You always know what is happening and can terminate the session on request at any time during the regression. My own experience, as well as that of experts who have studied hypnosis in detail, has determined that in most cases you will only go as far as your ethical and moral beliefs will allow under very deep hypnosis. If you aren't willing to go beyond a certain point when you are conscious, you won't be able to go past it when you are in a hypnotic trance. If the therapist suggests something that the client doesn't want to explore, the person will immediately come out of the trance.

For a regression, I place people in a trance that is light enough that they largely retain their critical awareness, yet is deep enough so the impressions out of the deepest past or from the spirit world can break through into consciousness. The client retains their inner beliefs and opinions in the trance and would immediately contradict the regression guide if the guide said something that didn't ring true. It's virtually impossible to lie to clients or lead healthy people where they don't want to go.

Conducting a Regression

During a regression, I try very hard to be aware of every client in their deepest being, so I put myself in a light trance, much lighter than what my client is in, so that I can have a better connection to them and the spirit world as I guide them through their regression. This also allows me to adjust myself to the client's individuality and recognize what they need. I am already in a light trance myself from the moment they walk in the door. I remain in this state of somewhat altered consciousness for the whole session right up to its conclusion. It would be almost impossible for me to work the way I do if I stayed completely in my everyday state of mind. I have everything structured in order to maintain the thread through the session. In a certain sense I retain control over the entire situation, but I stay in conscious connection with the spirit world, with my soul and my spirit guide, just as I do with the soul and the spirit guide of the client.

I have noticed that I often ask the client questions that I never could have come up with on my own. This intuitive knowing is also very helpful with people who don't want to admit to their true feelings. They might say, "I have absolutely no problems. Everything is okay and I am fine," but their tone of voice, facial expressions, and gestures radiate out to me and say something completely different. I might see that the person is simply angry and is holding it inside. Another might be close to tears and fighting the urge to cry. A great deal of information reveals itself to me in ways like these even before we start working on the regression process.

It's very important for me to work in a light trance state and so closely connected with the spirit world. This puts me in a position to let a higher wisdom and a deeper understanding flow into the session, appropriate to the particular person who is there. It sometimes astonishes me how I can act gently and carefully with some clients and very severely with others, with seemingly no apparent reason each time. And then it turns out that it was the right thing for those clients to hear at that precise moment in time and it helped them.

The Actual Regression

When the client has taken a place on the couch for their treatment and found a comfortable position, I begin with a physical relaxation sequence. This allows the client to quiet down and leave their everyday concerns behind. When they are ready, I begin with the visualization and lead the client into the first inner images. There are countless techniques for this, and I select the one that I think is best suited to the particular person. Someone might be having difficulties getting rid of their stress from the past few weeks, so I might guide this client to relax by visualizing lying down in a meadow of flowers. Those who are extremely anxious need to let their feelings become soft, loving, and peaceful. I might have them visualize a much-loved pet. When they have spent a few happy moments with it, they feel safe and comforted. Even if the client was very tense and troubled by the thought that they wouldn't be able to relax, they still gradually sink ever deeper into a trance.

Involving the Soul from the Beginning

Along with relaxation and protection, it's important from the start that the client is willing to work with a higher energy. It's something I discuss with clients right away. I make a point to use terms such as "cosmic light," "higher consciousness," and "divine light" because they are terms that are familiar to most people and are all-encompassing of spiritual beliefs.

It is just as important that clients tune in to clear and wise thoughts. Many clients feel very small and helpless, but if I use words such as "inner clarity" and "wisdom," they can quickly connect with those concepts. Ultimately it's my intention from the start to address and draw in the soul of the client through certain mental images and words and the sound of my voice.

I bring every client into contact with their spirit guide very early on in the regression process. This encounter feels like a gentle embrace or appears as a bright light. Achieving this sense of security and feeling of complete trust right away is very important for the success of the session.

A Springboard into a Past Life

Once the client is fully in a trance, I guide them back into early childhood. I use the early childhood as a kind of springboard into a past life. We have already clarified everything beforehand, so we are not trying to sort out any of the relationships from that earlier time or have the client experience a difficult event. The reason I go back to childhood by asking them to describe harmless things to me is so the client learns to move back in time and can tell me what they see. This also allows the client to respond to my questions just like I would like them to do during the past-life experience.

After the client has gone back to their childhood, we go back to the womb. This is a very interesting time, and even at this stage we can find out a great deal about the theme of the session. Many clients will know astonishingly well what they have planned for this life and what their goals and tasks are during this portion of the regression process. The way of knowing what is present at this stage in the womb is much more like the one that the person was used to when they lived as a soul.

The soul can move a short distance out of the little body in the mother's womb during pregnancy. However, it remains bound to the body, so that it can immediately return again if needed. Discovering this feeling of freedom as a grown person can be an important experience. The baby already possesses an earthly body, but it experiences itself much more strongly as a soul and knows all about life's larger context.

This phase of the regression reinforces the client's confidence that they already carry all the wisdom they will ever need, and that they know more than they think they do with the restrictions of their everyday self.

Despite her clearly very feminine body, one client presented herself like a man in her clothing, job, way of speaking, and way of moving. She was attracted to men and eventually wanted to have a relationship with a man that would go beyond being good friends. However, she wasn't comfortable with her femininity and was anxious about projecting herself as a woman. She wondered whether she shouldn't have been a man and whether something had gone wrong somewhere. In her regression, she realized that she wanted to be a woman when she was in the womb and that her gender today was not a mistake but a conscious decision. When she was in the womb, she was able to tell me that up until then, she had never incarnated as a woman. She had decided upon a woman's body for the first time, and despite her sense of joyful excitement, she realized in retrospect that she still felt very uncertain about this new role. Once she came to the conclusion that she had consciously chosen to be a woman, she was no longer afraid to express her femininity. She was more comfortable in her own skin and finally felt like she belonged and could truly embrace her true self.

After this interesting interlude in the womb, I take the client even further back and into a past life. One life is normally revealed during one session, which is usually sufficient for what the spirit guide wants the client to experience. Sometimes two or even a whole series of past lives where individual sequences seem to follow a specific theme can play out. The precise details that are shown depend on what is important for the client to learn from this regression and what they can handle at that moment in time. What is shown varies widely, but these events typically consist of high points, turning points, and significant sections from what happened in that specific person's life. Timewise, the events in that life may go back and forth. A person might initially experience life as a young man of twenty-three, then as a little boy of five, and finally as an old man of ninety-one.

After all these years of working as a spiritual regression therapist, I would venture to say that no therapist has ever been in a position to consciously choose a suitable life for their client. You wouldn't ever be able to arrange it so well, even for yourself.

Some clients will predict what they will experience during the session so that they can understand something better. They may think they already know the crucial theme, but then they discover that it's a completely different story during the regression. Sure, there are sometimes cases where the client already knew or suspected what was going to rise to the surface, but people in those situations are usually caught up in more superficial levels of thinking and feeling. The spirit world, the spirit guide, and the unity of the soul know very well what situation this person finds themselves in on Earth, how things are set up according to their overriding life plan, and what instructions they could benefit from most for their further evolution. Only then do they select the past life for that person.

chapter eight

In the Spirit World

When exploring a past life during a regression, I always go right to the end of that life with my client. We look at how the client died in the past and then I lead them into the spirit world, where they are met by their spirit guide. There we look back at the previous life that has just come to an end. The client, now in the guise of a soul, can let the stages of that life pass in review from a higher perspective and learn some lessons from it. The spirit guide stands beside the client and may offer comfort and sympathy or may deliver a genuine telling-off as well.

One client's past life wasn't that crucial, but the importance of the session was that the spirit guide was able to speak to her directly. He forced her to look at her laziness and her endless blaming of others. He said if she kept going like this, she would live a stunted and unsatisfied life, would learn nothing from it, and would not develop in the way that they had already decided on for this life. "It all lies within your power," he concluded.

I try to have my clients feel as intensely and thoroughly as they can the sense of what it is to be a soul while they are a guest in the spirit world and have a strong inner awareness. The connection with the spirit guide's divine energy can also play an important role in this. Just when I notice that someone is having problems with perceiving themselves as an exalted and wonderful consciousness or they do not value themselves highly enough to ask the higher energies for advice and guidance, I reunite them with their spirit guide. They experience what it's like to feel a loving higher energy and how to possess that in themselves. The energy of light, the sense of wellbeing from being embedded in a greater divine whole, and the joy that the client feels just from being in the spirit world completely surround and envelop the client. I then have them draw that feeling into their body, heart, and way of thinking so they can carry it into their current life. This personal experience leads to a direct positive transformation that can help people make great advances in their current life today.

At this point, the session is now moving gradually toward an end. I will often send the client back once again to a certain situation in their past life, one that we might have already looked at. Frequently, their existence back then had some properties or qualities that their current life lacks today. Perhaps they're currently an unfriendly curmudgeon and killjoy lost in lofty intellectual and philosophical thought, and back then they were not as sharp mentally but were still a joyful and grateful person. I then let the client feel this satisfaction with themselves and their life one more time, and take it deep within. They might discover that they do already possess this quality but had simply forgotten it. They can now reintegrate it into their daily life; it doesn't have to be cultivated all over again, but just remembered in that realm of feelings. Someone else might have absolutely no self-confidence, so I will have them refuel by going back to a past-life situation where they were utterly aware of all their power and strength.

I only finish a session once the client feels good and has the impression they have completed something and learned something.

This is the external format of a spiritual regression as I offer it. In reality, it can unfold in many possible directions. Sometimes the session has to be briefly interrupted halfway through. There are individual clients who can't stay in a trance that long and need a break. An interruption is possible and won't lessen the experience or lesson. I lead the client back into everyday reality, take a break, and then quickly lead them back to the place where we stopped.

The Aftermath of a Regression

Once the client is fully awake, more questions can then be clarified where necessary. Usually there aren't any more. The experience during a regression often affects clients so much that there are only a few people who will try to rationalize it right afterward. I also prefer that they avoid this because I want to prevent the client from tarnishing some of the deeper experiences and insights before shutting down again.

Once the client has fully returned to a state of normal daily consciousness, they are not prohibited from doing anything. They can get in their car, drive away, and resume their regular business. I do recommend that they have something to drink and, if hungry, to eat a little bit first, and maybe also go for a short walk. It is also highly recommended that clients make time to be alone after a session so that what they just experienced can be allowed to settle down a bit.

After a regression, clients should initially distance themselves from the inquisitive questions of any third parties. Regressions are very intimate and personal things, and for that reason I advise that clients share only what they really want to share with other people.

Do Regressions Always Work?

I have been very fortunate that the regressions that I have led myself have always succeeded. Naturally I cannot give a guarantee that this will always be the case. I also cannot claim that all my clients' expectations have been fulfilled as they expected them to be.

What does "succeed" mean in this context? To illustrate this, I would like to describe a client who had just completed a long flight in order to attend a regression appointment with me. He was jetlagged but thought that didn't matter because he hadn't slept properly in months and in his opinion was not far off from having a heart attack. He was trembling and all over the place to an extent that I had never seen before. He was very nice and quite young, a top manager and stressed to the highest degree. Even in our opening conversation he was using two cell phones, one on the left ear and one on the right. Without pausing for breath, he gave advice and information, responded to questions, and made decisions. I was very curious about what was most likely to come up in our session.

He spoke very good English, but as soon as he was in a trance, he lapsed into an English dialect that I could only understand with difficulty. I actually didn't have to try to understand him for too long, as he fell asleep straight away when he was put into a deeper trance. I woke him up because he hadn't come to me for sleep. Because of that he gave a start, and as a result he was wide awake once more. I had to start all over again and lead him back into a trance, and when he got there, he fell asleep again immediately.

This routine repeated itself a number of times. At some point when he was awake again, I told him that this was pointless and that it was important he learn how to relax properly in his life. Once he was properly rested and was wide awake again, he could then start to think about his lifestyle. In this instance he didn't need an actual regression in order to make the necessary lifestyle changes.

So was this a successful session? At first glance, of course not. However, if he looked at what happened with only half-opened eyes and only took it half-seriously, it could have presented him with an entirely new outlook on his life, and I consider that a success. It might have been the most important consultation of his life! Even if he had only slept there, ultimately it might even have saved his life. A spirit guide once had a very particular piece of advice prepared for a very results-oriented man: "The greatest achievement that you can accomplish is to accomplish less."

A session is a success if it brings something positive for the client in terms of self-awareness and consciousness expansion, regardless of how many past-life images they were actually able to see. In the end, the important question is, What will my next steps in life look like?

Felizitas, one of my clients, traveled a long way to be guided back into a past life. She had saved up for it for a long time and was here at last. She experienced a past life, but relatively little information came out of it and there was nothing remarkable about it in any way. Felizitas, however, was thrilled, and she raved about how much she was now able to understand, what she still had to learn, and all the things she now wanted to change in her life.

A year later she made an appointment to have another regression consultation, as she had the feeling that she had now implemented everything that she had been shown the first time. When we met again, I saw a completely changed woman standing before me. She had indeed implemented it all! We did another regression and again I had the feeling that nothing spectacular was going to happen during it, but again Felizitas was utterly fascinated and overjoyed by all the new things that came to her. She recognized then that it was all a question of joy.

A whole year went by before she got in touch with me again. We arranged another appointment, and once again she was completely changed. She was like a blaze of bright sunshine when she arrived at my doorstep. She was radiant with joie de vivre and vitality. Her life had become even brighter and more attractive since she had integrated into her life all the experiences from her last session and had focused entirely on joy.

I would say that out of all my clients whom I was able to accompany into a past life, Felizitas had gone through the greatest changes in the shortest time. Her example shows very clearly that in a regression it does not matter whether a session unfolds in a spectacular fashion; the only thing that matters is what the person makes of it.

For many people, the regression is easy and they have no difficulty sending their consciousness on a journey back in time, opening up and letting things happen. On the other hand, it can be tougher for other people, and some have to try harder right from the start of the session. Some people pick up a lot of information and others less. But whatever does happen (and assuming that the regression guide is up to standard and that the client really does want to do a regression and isn't doing it for someone else's sake), it is ultimately something that is going to help this person in their life today.

It is a wonder that inside a space of three or four hours something so great can happen to us. If we accept this with gratitude and joy and make the best of it, we can gain an enormous amount of wisdom for our personal benefit.

chapter nine

Regression as a Profound Experience

While in a trance, clients experience events in their consciousness both in the present and in the past. As a person living today, they are aware that they are currently undergoing a regression procedure and are watching events from the past. On the other hand, they are experiencing life as the person they were in the past life, and in that past life they obviously don't know that their life is being considered again decades, centuries, or even millennia later.

How strongly the client is conscious of their present-day awareness in one of the other time locations varies according to the session. And of course the depth of the penetration into the consciousness of the past can also be controlled. Thus it can be very helpful in some cases to remind the client of the everyday awareness they have in the life now when they might be steering their attention toward a situation in the past life that happens to be causing them anxiety. I will then calm them down and remind them that they are only watching it all with a part of their current attention, that it is in the past, and that it can't harm them anymore—they are lying here safe and secure.

Finding Yourself Back in a Past Life

Sometimes it takes little while before a client appears in the events of the past. It might happen that they are describing the wild tumult of battle, but they are watching it from a distance. Slowly they become aware that they are in the midst of it themselves, wielding a sword. They now realize that they are a part of it: they fight, they wound, they kill, they are in danger. Or a client finds herself back in ancient Greece. There she sees all the people wearing long, flowing robes and then suddenly discovers she is wearing a miniskirt and sunglasses and gets the impression that something isn't right. Then a bit later she notices, "Aha, now I too am wearing a flowing robe like that." At last she has managed to make that jump in time.

How the individual perceives this information in the past life can vary a great deal, just as it can in their life today. Some things you just know, and you don't need to ponder them too much. Other things are conveyed using a powerful feeling, and sometimes there will be images standing right there in the foreground. It's almost always a mixture of all of these. If someone likes a particular landscape and thinks about it, a mental image of it will appear before their inner eye. If someone has just fallen in love, that feeling will be very present with them. If on the other hand someone is asked for their name or date of birth, barely any image or feeling will arise, but they will be able to give the answer without having to think about it.

Almost everyone sees images and experiences feelings in the trance, and it's as if what they perceive there has really just happened in that moment. In this state of consciousness every person gets images, but the person is not always aware of this immediately. A client could say, "No, I can't see anything. But there is a white single-story house with a red roof and green shutters." If I were then to inquire, "So you don't see anything, but there is a house with a green roof," then the person might even correct me: "No, the roof is red."

During the regression, the client gives names to things as they appear to them; to mull them over too much would be neither sensible nor helpful and should be avoided at all costs. Initially there just won't be any evidence that something you experience is true or isn't true unless you feel like doing some research later and manage to verify some aspects of your experience. After all, you don't look for verifiable evidence in your everyday life; you just trust that the facts concerning your personal history are true. No one ever questions their own name or address.

Experiencing a Past Life with All Your Senses

During a regression, a person experiences what's happening with all their senses, so it isn't just guided by what they see. For example, if they eat an apple, they will taste it as well. One client shouted out, completely beside herself, "Ugh, what a smell! That's horrible!" I asked her about it, and she explained that she was in a tannery. Her face was screwed up in disgust. Inwardly she was completely alive in those past-life events.

Pain can also arise, albeit in a significantly diminished form. Someone can experience a punch to the head. They might feel this pain a little, but not as strongly as they would in the "real version" of the events. In these cases, the soul will distance itself automatically from the experience.

When you are experiencing a previous existence, you will laugh and cry, just as you do in your current life. You get angry, you enjoy yourself, you get worried, and you get bored. It's all dependent upon what you experience and how you assess it for yourself. These are real feelings and their manifestations.

Very rarely have I come across clients who can watch the whole thing completely without experiencing any feelings to a degree beyond a healthy level of self-protection. That could be a sign of how much the person is suppressing their feelings in their current life and thus how important it would be if they could learn to start admitting them again. Right now they have no access to them and therefore can't pick up on the feelings that belong to their past life either. Maybe this person has been brought up in their current existence so that they have to behave in a particularly "manly" way, or they suppress their feelings so they don't get hurt or don't feel their old wounds. In this scenario they might even be experiencing life in a dungeon, knowing that everything around them is horrible, but they won't feel that. They can also observe beautiful scenes completely without having any feelings about them.

In rare cases it's actually a good thing to remember certain events from a previous life without emotion. The client is watching it all as if from a higher perspective. They don't need to immerse themselves deeper into the feelings because they would only get unnecessarily lost in their emotions instead of paying attention to the fundamental issues that lie behind them, which are much more essential for their current life.

For me as a regression guide, the moment when I have to decide whether or not I should bring the client into contact with their feelings is sometimes quite tricky. Then it's important for me to turn to the spirit world with a request for advice. With this guidance I can draw the appropriate conclusions so I can lead the regression in a manner that brings the best possible help for the client.

When the Current Life Sets Limits

The knowledge and ability to perceive and communicate verbally what we possess in our life today can have a great influence on how we reexperience earlier existences. It can be that someone today is rather uneducated and barely in a position to express themselves. Perhaps in an earlier life they were a highly educated and musically gifted person. Now when I lead them to a regression into this past life, they can only perceive in a vague sense how things were for them then and can only share this in a limited way. The fineness or the coarseness of their senses today simply puts limits on them.

Usually it is the case that you can experience the feelings from the past very clearly, even if during your life today you are not very well tuned in to them. Even a jaded cynic can experience the thoroughly exuberant vitality of a past existence and let some of that flow into their life today.

A man who paid a great deal of attention to discipline, strictness, and consistency for himself and for his children and who placed the utmost importance on knowing a lot and being an upright person in society experienced a past life as a small child in an orphanage. The client could feel his feelings from those days very clearly. He had food to eat and a roof over his head, but he suffered terribly from the absence of human warmth and loving affection. When he was only seven years old, he drowned in a stream. It was clear to the soul, once back in the spirit world, that it wanted to learn in that life how it feels for a child to be emotionally self-sufficient. It became clear to this man that security is much more important than pure knowledge and outward tidiness. This was an important lesson for him in terms of his life today and the raising of his children.

From my experience, I can say that by the end of a regression consultation a clear picture always emerges. A whole life is open like the pages of a book: the events, the circumstances, a personality, and its feelings, character, and destiny.

Experiencing Your Own Death

In every regression consultation I accompany my clients right up to their death in a past life and then beyond. This can, at least to a certain extent, take away the fear of death that they might have in this present life. Through this reliving of death, they are able to grasp that nothing on Earth lasts forever, everything passes, and that despite it all, they do exist eternally as a soul, which is indestructible and happy.

Many people can't get over the death of a beloved family member. A suicidal woman came to me for help. Her husband of many years had died and she wanted to follow him, but because she had four elderly dogs, she wanted to live until they died before joining her husband.

In her past life she could see herself again as a widow who had been withdrawn from life for thirty years and had vegetated alone, joyless and haggard. She was happy when she finally died and could return to the spirit world. There she met the soul of her beloved, who was her husband in her past life and also in the life she was living now. This soul told her very forcefully: "It had been arranged that I would leave before you. It's because you wanted to learn to deal in a positive way with a life on your own at last and also to find joy and a meaning to life without me. Please don't make the same mistake again! I have already tried many times to let you know this, but your sorrow has always gotten in the way of me reaching you." This had a profound effect on the woman. I later found out she moved to Spain and was living on a pension with her dogs. She adopted two more young dogs rescued from cruelty and was all ready to enjoy a fulfilling retirement.

Death can be experienced in very different ways, depending on the circumstances. Once the soul has left the body and part of it has entered the spirit world, everything is fine for all my clients and they will affirm: "I am at home here and not there on Earth. On Earth it's as if I am a guest, and here, in the spirit world, I am at home." We are eternal divine souls that feel like they are people when they are on Earth and for the most part have forgotten who they truly are. We are most certainly not people who have to work at transforming ourselves into souls!

In some cases clients worry about those who will be left behind, which can overwhelm the dying person. If a person is still characterized by hatred, greed, or revenge, leaving their earthly existence will also feel rather tough.

The Actual Death

In a regression we usually don't dwell at the actual place of death for very long. A client might tell me that they are lying in bed old and ill, that everything hurts, that they are alone and afraid, and that everything is horrible. Then in the very next moment they are already rejoicing because they have an awareness of themselves as a soul, floating and free. If it's all happening too quickly, I ask the client just to return again and really pay attention to what happens in the moment of death. Most of them can reconstruct exactly how they leave the body. Some souls leave it as if through a whirlpool above the head or the chest. Others feel as if they just stand up and walk away, and only then do they notice that their physical body didn't stand up with them but is still lying there.

If someone finds the act of dying difficult, it's almost always because they don't want to go and are clinging to life on Earth and to their body. Once they can feel the lightness and freedom, no one wants to go back. In this moment they have let go.

After the many regressions that I have gone through myself both as a client and as a guide, I can say that dying seems much easier than being born.

Difficult Transitions

When a client has left their body behind in a previous life, I give them time to say their farewells. Some would like to go back to their body one more time, and others want to go quickly back to a loved one or an animal to which they were close. This can also be someone whom they didn't have any contact with for many years. Many also want to see a landscape one last time or an old neighborhood that meant a lot to them.

If someone was killed in battle or in an argument, sometimes they want to take a quick look at how it unfolded. Then this feeling often prevails: "My God, how pointless and horrible this all is! There are no winners. Everyone here loses, even those who think they are the winners."

There are also cases in which someone suddenly realizes at the moment of death what a horrible person they really were. They can then be seized by feelings of guilt and remorse, and that can make for a difficult crossing over because the dark clouds can go on for quite some time, blocking off the view across the breadth of Heaven.

Some of the recently deceased initially still feel somewhat heavy or tired. They may have difficulty accepting their own death or are interested for some time to come in what happened next to their body. For example, they watch their own funeral. There are also souls who continue to stay back because they feel they are a failure and are embarrassed about their past behavior.

Some souls become almost overwhelmed by the grief of those left behind, who might be gathered around the dead body and who don't want to let their beloved relative or friend go. The deceased person will often try to make contact with their relative and say to them, "I am still around. I am not dead. I am fine. There's no need to be sad." Usually the living don't notice the person—their pain and grief have made them blind—and that too can make it harder for the deceased to disengage from the situation.

Some souls stay long enough on Earth so they know the bereaved are properly cared for and comforted. It can sometimes happen that the soul of the deceased is granted a brief glimpse into the relative's future. These souls would like their bereaved friends and relatives to be doing well.

Ultimately every soul is drawn back up to the spirit world because they grasp that earthly life is a matter for others and they no longer bear any responsibility for that life. When this insight takes a bit longer to come and someone is finding it very hard to pull away from Earth, there will soon be a spiritual being on hand to help them move on.

Once people are experiencing their existence more as a soul and have cast off earthly things, they find that they have a whole different mode of perception. They then have a greater overview and a much deeper level of knowledge about things. They don't worry what will become of the people left behind on Earth. They simply know that every soul has chosen their mission as a human and that everything has been put at their disposal so they can go on to achieve it. They have no doubt that they will see those people they have a deep connection with again. And they know that everything that happens on Earth, every outcome and test they experience, is embedded in a much larger context.

When the time comes, partners in love will meet each other again in the spirit world. But until then, for as long as one of them is still on Earth, it's not necessary—and it's not even desired by the soul of the one who has died—that the beloved other shouldn't enter into any new relationships. No soul demands loyalty beyond physical death.

A widower who suffered from loneliness after the death of his wife and withdrew completely from his life experienced a past life as a dying woman who was leaving behind a husband and two children. It was of great concern to her how things would go for her family after her death, and she hoped very much that her husband would be happy and would also find another good partner. After this my client said, "I always had the feeling that it would hurt Elsbeth if I stopped grieving for her. What a crazy idea! She definitely wants things to go well for me. It must be tough for her to see me suffer for so long."

The Experience of Being a Soul

In most cases the soul of the deceased is drawn away from Earth by some force after a relatively short time. Most people experience this as a pleasant sense of being drawn away.

Clients then describe how they change form. Most people say that at first they look like they did in life, but much younger and fresher. Sometime later they experience that form dissolving and they become like a kind of cloud, a colorful sphere of light. Others see themselves in angelic form.

Most people can decipher other presences that receive and welcome them. At that point these presences can have the outward appearance of people they knew on Earth. I have discovered through some careful investigation that they don't have fixed physical forms but look enough like they did on Earth so that the recently dead person can recognize them. These can be friends, relatives, or acquaintances. Often they are the other members of the client's soul group, who have been together over a long period of time. These beings sometimes weren't particularly close to the person who has just come back. Perhaps they weren't even incarnated during that person's lifetime. They knew each other, though, during the life between lives and other past lives and are deeply connected to each other.

In most cases these reunions and the fresh return into the spirit world are characterized by great joy. The returning soul becomes aware that a dense veil of forgetfulness had been placed over it, which has now disappeared again. When the soul has taken this road to return above, difficulties and pain, sadness and fear, and all feuds and doubts fall away from it, and the soul experiences itself as free and happy.

In fact, when they return to the spirit world after their death experience, every client goes through this wonderful period of freedom from all earthly cares and pains. Only later, once they have taken a look once more at their past life from this different sphere and might then get the feeling that they got some things wrong, can regret start to set in: "Oh no, my behavior on Earth wasn't all that good! I didn't recognize or fulfill my life tasks."

One client was a warrior in his past life. He was very good at hand-to-hand combat and killed many people. He felt happiest when he was truly in the midst of his rage for blood, his veins full of adrenaline and in full command of all his powers. He also enjoyed feeling so light and free after his death. He was proud of the life he had lived, which he had mastered using his power and courage. With this as his belief, he returned to the spirit world. All the people he had killed were lined up there to greet him. They were absolutely quiet and at peace. He started to become ever smaller as he moved step by step past this row of people. He had to wonder, "What have I really done? Does the meaning of life consist of cutting other people's heads off and stabbing them through the heart?" He reached the end of the long line. His spirit guide was there and greeted him with the words "welcome home."

There are just a few souls for whom this lightness and joy are clouded, who state that it's really not going so well for them as souls. They are profoundly damaged because a great deal was done to them in a tough and draining life on Earth or because they did the same to others. It is important for these souls first of all to seek out a place of regeneration and recovery in the spirit world. I will also go to those places with clients in this position. The soul will be purified and healed using various ways and means. After that, these clients feel ready to look back once more to the earthly life that has just been completed. They now have the strength for this review.

The Review of the Past Life

This is a significant part of the regression process. Through this kind of review, made from a higher state of consciousness and in the company of the spirit guide, it is possible for the client to recognize properly what their strengths and weaknesses were in that life and what they should learn from those images for their life today. That past life was shown to them during that session for a particular reason. I also try to get to this review with the clients as quickly as possible, for if they remain for too long in that state of bliss as a soul, it can then happen that their remorse for some poor behavior in a past life can fade so far into the background that they don't want to deal with it anymore. Then it becomes difficult to draw the relevant lessons out of it for their current life.

During the review of the past life, the client's feelings can vary considerably. Some souls are appalled by their selfish and unkind behavior on Earth. Others will claim that they have given a pretty good account of themselves, possibly better than it actually seemed during that life. Perhaps someone will notice with a surprise, "I finally got it right! At last I have learned to make a proper commitment to my wife and children. I found it very hard and sometimes I also didn't look on it as anything particularly significant. But I did keep trying across many lifetimes and I had yet to succeed, and I always drifted away from them—and so this time I was able to do it. What a fantastic outcome!"

Or someone might come to this review after their life on Earth and have the feeling of not having achieved enough academically, despite having good teachers. As a soul, they might recognize that until then they had worked as a farmer or a manual laborer and that achievements on a mental level were new territory for them. They might think, "That's why I performed pretty well. That's why I did a valiant job with what I had!" In many cases your own judgment about how the newly completed life went gets moderated because you can now get a view from a much higher level and a wider significance is apparent at last.

But the opposite can also happen: you might have found it a wonderful life yourself, but then you have to admit as a soul, "Unfortunately that wasn't quite so great." For example, someone might come back after an earthly life, which seemed to go pretty well, and stand before their spirit guide, who is looking serious. The soul slowly remembers: "Yes, this time I wanted to learn not to get lost in worldly things and to keep incorporating the spiritual into what I did, even though I had very materialistic parents. I was a monk twice, and a hermit once, and a nun once, and all that went well. And now I wanted to experience how I could live in the midst of all the worldly turmoil, but I completely forgot that."

Or someone might initially be very satisfied because they never rebelled, but were always very submissive toward authority figures, their parents, and their spouse. They gradually see that they could have demanded a great deal more of themselves and could have evolved much more. Although they did nothing bad, they were too accommodating and timid, did not live up to their potential in any way, and didn't tackle any of the issues for which they had gone to Earth.

At forty-five years old, one client of mine felt ancient: "I am definitely not living, and I could be eighty or already dead." She was completely bogged down by feelings of guilt and couldn't appreciate anything pleasurable. When she actually managed at last to make plans to go to the cinema, her husband stopped her because he wanted to sit at home every evening and wanted her there with him. In her past life, this woman saw how she had spent all her time caring for her very demanding parents, for whom she'd had to be there twenty-four hours a day. They had forbidden her from having any friends and certainly no boyfriend. She hadn't been allowed to go out and or buy anything nice to wear. The local priest, who had been the family's only friend, had rebuked her when she spoke on one occasion of her longing for a life outside of the home. That was considered a sin, and her job was to be there with her parents. The woman wasted away and died at age fifty, shortly after her parents' deaths. She then had to recognize in the spirit world that it had been her mission to stand up for herself and her needs. The client could not fail to notice very clearly the horror of this wasted life, and a newly rebellious energy was now palpable as it emerged in her.

There's another thing that clients realize is very significant as they go through the regression process and especially when they are in the spirit world: many difficulties and problems that we grapple with in our earthly lives can't be solved in this life because we lack the necessary overview of the larger meaning. When we try, we end up running around in circles. Every problem can be solved on a higher level because there are other options available for dealing with it. The client can also see their current life, which they have perhaps been struggling with, in a different light. They realize that they came into this world of their own free will, and they wanted their current existence to be exactly the way it is. They then see the problems that arise in their life as challenges that they will eventually master, which helps them evolve.

One client had great difficulty acknowledging other people. In a past life he had been a priest. He had been a decent person and had died at an advanced age. During his account, I got the feeling that he had been a very good social worker who had campaigned for the material well-being of his parishioners, but he seemed to lack all the other qualities that make one a good priest.

During the review, his spirit guide led him back to the church and helped him recall a great mystical experience he'd had when he was alive. The question came up of how he had dealt with this experience as a man of the cloth and whether he had shared what he had gone through with the community. He had to admit now, as a soul, that he had wanted to keep such experiences for himself and had made no attempt to share them with others. "I keep God to myself alone" was one of his inner statements during that life! He had felt that such an experience wasn't really for common people, and he hadn't wanted to diminish what he had gone through there.

When I asked him how, as a soul, he evaluated this, he said gloomily, "I completely missed my calling! The divine energy was not going to diminish. It doesn't become any less powerful when you share it with others."

First Steps in Your "New" Everyday Life

Right after a session, most people are, first of all, really pleased that it worked. They are almost always in a blissful state of wonder because of everything they went through. They feel renewed and full of potential.

Then they realize just how tired they are. Only a few feel more alert and energetic straight away. Although it may appear that they have just been lying there during the regression and not really doing anything, they do notice afterward that it has been an emotionally and mentally demanding experience. Their body and their whole being must first assimilate these new, or rather very old, experiences and also deal with the fact that more energy than usual is circulating through the body. This shouldn't be underestimated. Many people report back to me later that on the day of the regression they went to bed very early and slept for a long time. Body and mind take a well-deserved rest. Once this initial feeling of exhaustion is gone, most clients feel very lively, fresh, and strengthened. They feel comforted and newly connected with something greater.

Some people want to paint or draw something at the end of the session so they can express themselves. Perhaps they saw a symbol on the soul level during the session that will be helpful with the realization of their agenda. Others receive an exercise from their spirit guide, which they might want to try out during the period that follows. Some choose to listen to the audio recording of the session. In this way, they keep discovering new things that turn out to be significant. It is important not to listen to the recording when driving, as the trance instructions can still work even then!

Initial Processing of a Regression

After the regression comes a return to the daily routine. This is when you will find out what the experience has done for the client, but also what the client is ready to do with what they experienced. Many are bursting with ideas about all the things they want to tackle and change in their life. In every case, it's recommended that the client let everything settle down, at least initially, and not rush into anything. There'll often be a detail that suddenly comes to mind, when the person is completely relaxed; it's as if a jigsaw piece falls into place and the client understands the whole picture on an even deeper level.

The need to talk about what was experienced can vary. In this respect, clients should be very careful and trust their instincts. Sometimes friends or family members might pressure a person to share details of what happened out of curiosity. This should be resisted. Experiences should only be shared with trusted friends and are not an appropriate topic for a chat over coffee or a quick exchange of gossip.

In many cases, clients won't want to talk but rather will want to let a new internal balance develop. There are directions in therapy that sternly forbid talking about one's experiences for at least six weeks, but I prefer to leave it up to the client. If they follow their own instincts, they will remain silent about it for exactly the amount of time that's right for them. In my experience, most people don't want to talk about it anyway. After a regression, they are more focused on themselves and carry their experience inside them.

How Often Should One Undergo Regression?

Regressions in the way that I offer them shouldn't be undergone too often. It is not sensible to want to consume them in any kind of way like fast food, no matter how exciting they might be at first. It is recommended to start with a regression procedure that takes you into a past life. Then you can go to a further past life starting at the earliest one a day later, and from that point you can then make a visit to the life between lives. By that time, you will have so much material for further processing that you will have plenty to keep you occupied. When you get the feeling that you have inwardly processed and implemented all the experiences in a session, it can be very helpful to take part in a further regression.

I went through more than seventy regression procedures into past lives as a client. Only then did I get the feeling that it was finally enough, and I went on to concentrate more on spiritual regressions into the life between lives.

chapter ten

Step by Step

After a regression session, it's important that you process and then implement what you have learned and experienced on an interior level. Many people expect magnificent things to happen after a regression consultation. In doing so, they may overlook the fact that it can be the smaller steps they take that go on to change and improve their existence. Someone might recall that in a past life they were a genuine nature lover who could quite contentedly lie in a meadow or under a tree. The client knows that it can also do them good to be in nature in this life today. Despite that, they realize that it's been more than five years since they last left the city. This person might be unhappy, hunched in front of the television, drinking beer, and feeling more and more dissatisfied. They can discover through a regression that it could be so simple for them to live more joyfully again, that ultimately they might need nothing more than to visit nature—just as they did in that past life. They also need to make an immediate resolution: "This next week I will take two days' vacation and take a trip to the mountains." That may not sound like much, but it could change the person's whole life.

Picking up on small hints from a past life and taking them seriously is the challenge and the gift that a regression procedure can give us. It's a question of going deep into the experiences you have gained, of getting properly involved in it and of living it.

Good books or courses on the subject of spirituality and a positive lifestyle are also very helpful for staying on the ball. Life in our thoroughly organized and overly technical world has a tendency to lull us back very quickly into our mindless daily routine, if we don't keep consciously steering ourselves away from it. During a regression, a person comes face to face in a very direct way with their soul and makes contact with the spirit world, as well as with their spirit guide, who is always there for them. This is something that has to be kept in mind and constantly reinforced; the client has to keep refreshing their contact with these other levels, as well as reestablishing and broadening that connection.

We don't have to occupy ourselves solely with spiritual thoughts. For many people, it can be more important to dance more, listen to music, joyfully celebrate food, or take a painting class. The sensual pleasures that we discover and enjoy mindfully here on Earth are very important for our further evolution and don't lead us away from the spiritual path.

Living at All Times and on All Continents

In a regression procedure into a past life, people will find themselves in various different times and cultures. Now and then it can also be the case that someone has the experience of not even being on Earth but of being somewhere utterly different. This is rare and is not the subject of this book, but it is possible. In general, souls are free to incarnate in any country and at any time; however, many do have certain preferences that will be given priority.

Sometimes a client will experience a life in prehistoric times. Perhaps they become aware of what it's like to wield a club and hunt in a forest wearing an animal skin. Perhaps a mammoth will pass by. Such cases are fascinating because they feel very foreign compared to what we experience today and how we normally classify things. But at the same time they feel totally real while they are being experienced.

I am constantly amazed by the detailed accounts that I hear out of my clients' mouths, while they are clearly aware that in the life they are living today they have never been to those locations. During a session they will report back to me details that often can be verified as true through subsequent investigation.

When it comes to verifying the experiences of a regression, you must select past lives that don't lie too far back in the past. Otherwise you won't be able to find the things the clients described in those places anymore. Perhaps some clients have gotten the impression from documentaries or books that Middle Europeans have lived all their past lives in Middle Europe and in the past three hundred years. This is not true. Ultimately past lives in Middle Europe do form the majority for Middle Europeans of today, but that does not mean they might not have had lives in India or America as well. Yet what is relevant and still awaiting clarification for one's current life is usually to be found in the immediate geographical environment and in the last three or four centuries.

Inexplicable Attractions or Aversions

Sometimes clients will feel attracted in an inexplicably powerful way to a certain country or culture—and then it will turn out that they actually had a deeply formative past life there. Others will describe their great abhorrence for a country, even though they were never there and can't name any apparent reason for this aversion. In the regression it can then sometimes come to light that they spent a horrible past life in this exact country, the depths of which have not yet been worked through. Often, however, such an aversion or fascination doesn't have any actual relevance to the regression. All too often, expectations of this kind are left completely unfulfilled, so it doesn't really make sense to read too deeply into these things.

I have found that some people, during their regression, land in exactly the same place in which they are living now. This can be hard for them to accept at first. It's confusing; they think they have done something wrong, until they realize that they are indeed in the same place, but it's a completely different time. If they can let themselves go, this offers them a very exciting experience. They can see all the changes as they take place through time.

As a fascinating side effect, I have formulated a colorful interior kaleidoscope during my years as a regression therapist embracing all sorts of historical associations around the world. For example, I am forever finding out fascinating details about the technical and artistic skills of people from every conceivable culture. I can also trace changes on Earth by combining all the various data that I've collected during all the regressions. I once had a client who was experiencing himself as a woman in an Arabian harem. He was able to tell me the exact region he was living in then and insisted that it was wonderfully green there. I knew, though, that today this is a desert region. After the session I did a bit of investigating, and I found out that the place where his past life had taken place really was, at that time, a luscious and fertile landscape.

The man who experienced himself as a woman in the aforementioned harem was incidentally very happy there. He described how wonderfully the women all understood one another and in what a colorful, easy, and joyful manner his life there had unfolded. He was surprised by that, as in his current life he was an almost dogged defender of monogamy and of the typical Middle European family.

Regression: A Foolhardy Undertaking?

Reliving an earlier existence is, for most people, something so astonishing and far from the ordinary in every respect that some fears can start to develop around it. I can only speak of what I have discovered for myself during regressions I have gone through, in my training and later in my many years of work with my own clients. Yet I can say this about it quite unequivocally: a spiritual regression is, when properly handled, a great blessing. Of course, along with regression, there are many other methods for furthering one's spiritual evolution. Every person will find themselves at a different point on their own path, and the same technique is not right and appropriate for everyone.

There are a few preconditions that will help clients get the most from the process. The regression therapist is a crucial factor. This person must be well positioned to assess what is right and appropriate for every client. The client must also be properly prepared for the experience. They have to be honest in the preliminary conversation. They shouldn't be taking drugs or be on heavy medication, they shouldn't be under the influence of alcohol, and they mustn't have any serious psychological problems.

In the case of psychological disturbances or some physical illnesses, it's necessary that the client discuss it beforehand with their doctor or psychotherapist, preferably one who knows about regressions and who is generally well disposed toward them.

If clients don't pay proper heed to this, regressions could be dangerous. In most cases the soul's self-protection would still come into play. The person concerned would simply not experience very much, would hardly see any images, and would not get involved in any dramatic scenes from their past lives, if they weren't able to stand them. This level of security will be in place if the past life has been chosen by the spirit world.

As soon as one client of mine saw that she had been raped in a past life, she was able to speak freely. This had also happened to her in her current life, six years prior, at age thirteen. She hadn't spoken to anyone about it, as the perpetrator was a relative. It was made very apparent to her during the session that she now had to stand up for herself and make sure the man was held accountable for his actions. Only then would she be able to process and let go of it all so that she wouldn't waste anymore of her life in a state of grief, shame, and self-reproach.

One question that clients often ask is, What happens if someone can't find their way back from a past life? There's a clear answer to that: it doesn't happen. In all proper literature as well as in my own experiences and in those of many other therapists, I don't know of one single case in which someone hasn't found their way back. Even if the therapist had a heart attack in the middle of the session or even died, the client would simply drop off to sleep after a short time, wake up, and find themselves back in their current life. In such drastic and highly improbable cases, it could be therapeutically necessary to work through the rest of the interrupted session to its conclusion with another regression guide.

Tragic Events in a Past Life

Many people are afraid they might encounter an unpleasant or otherwise bad situation in their regression that might overwhelm them. This fear is unnecessary in a properly guided spiritual regression. The spirit guide will only show someone what they can easily deal with and what provides a positive benefit for their life today.

Even if the situation in the past life was so bad that it cost the person their life in a dreadful manner, the client will have no problem reliving it today in their trance: a part of them will always remain in the position of spectator and thus maintain a certain distance from it. Someone can experience having a knife stuck in their chest; it is more a knowing, rather than sensing the actual pain from it. It's a bit like watching a terrifying scene on television: you enter fully into the situation, but you also know at the same time that it's only a film and that you are actually sitting comfortably on the sofa. In exactly the same way, the client also knows that what's being experienced is from the past and they are safe and sound, held within their body from today.

As the regression guide, I usually conduct the client quickly through unpleasant situations. There is no point in lingering there any longer than necessary. There are many possible ways to make it easier for the client. For example, I can at first let them observe the dramatic scene from a bit further away as a spectator, or lead them backward or forward in time to a moment in the corresponding life where things are going better for them. When they have recovered and relaxed a little, we can go back to the tricky moment so that it can be felt and processed properly. Renewed contact with the spirit guide can also be very helpful. With the guide's help, the client can go back with a sense of security to what was causing them fear, and once they are back in that situation, there will no longer be any fear. What remains is to experience and process the situation.

If necessary, I can help the client desensitize themselves specifically from stressful emotions so they can't have a negative influence on their current life any longer. The client will still know all about what happened, but it won't burden them anymore.

Critical voices will still enjoy plucking out examples of people who were no longer able to cope with life after a regression. They might give an example of someone who experienced an existence as a murderer and consequently suffers from considerable feelings of guilt. Something like that can only happen if an inexperienced and incompetent therapist is conducting the regression. I myself have never witnessed someone have difficulty accepting themselves in this role afterward. On the contrary, an unpleasant memory from a past life would only be shown to a client so that things could be better for them in their current life. That is what the evaluation with the spirit guide is for. Unfortunately, a number of regression therapists let this part of the work slide. I would never release a client from a session until all their questions had been clarified and until it feels calm on all sides and good for them and for me.

As I ask the spirit world to choose the particular past life and corresponding scenes, I leave the protective function of the soul all the room it needs, and the client then will only ever be shown the events that it can properly assimilate at that precise moment in time. If you pay heed to that, the client will never feel overwhelmed. They will instinctively sense and understand why and how they can use this past life as a vital source of guidance for their current life.

chapter eleven

What Matters Most

A spiritual regression is a tremendous opportunity for growth and a great and unique gift. In the hands of a competent regression guide with integrity, it is something strengthening, purifying, and comforting. These qualities of a regression therapist are not something to be underestimated. They are the prerequisite for a successful session. A regression is in absolutely no way something that a person can try out with whoever happens to be nearby, if only for the simple reason that the person could become very opened up and thus irritated or injured. Regression needs to be taken seriously as a technique and as an opportunity for growth. It is not a toy. If someone claims to be a regression guide, be sure to confirm that they have the corresponding in-depth training and technical skill.

This actual technique and its serious application are essential for a regression. I myself experienced my first regression in the same way as most people in that it basically stopped after death. What was missing was the placing of everything into the context of a greater whole, the encounter with the spirit guide, the experience of being in the spirit world, and the realization that all this was to be used in my current life. When a regression happens in the way it did for me then, it can easily result in the client feeling confused after the session, with more issues than they had before.

Closely related to the question of the technique is the question of the personality of the one who's employing it. In all events you need an experienced and inwardly mature regression guide. Without doubt there is quite a lot required to lead a person into a past life so they can draw a great spiritual and therapeutic use out of it. It has to be a calling from the heart and not just a job. You should have at your disposal a well-grounded training and experience, initially as a client and then as a regression guide. You must be able to deal sensibly with all the clients' questions, head off all their uncertainties and fears, and adequately consider and evaluate all their experiences and sensations as they emerge during a session.

People keep coming to me for advice when they want to undergo training as a regression guide, despite the fact that they themselves have never undergone a regression as a client. That seems to me a bit like someone wanting to receive training as a ski instructor when they haven't even stood on skis. I would recommend to everyone before they seriously consider training as a regression guide that they at the very least undergo an initial forty sessions with various different regression guides who work with as many different techniques as possible. If after that you really want to lead regressions for yourself, you should find a sound training program. A serious training, in my eyes, will definitely take a whole lot longer than just a few weekends!

There are countless methods for placing someone in a trance. After some practice it is quite easy to do. The following is the most important consideration: What do you then do with the person who is lying before you in a trance? This is where it starts to get interesting. Of course you might already have learned a great deal about this. You should indeed have learned a great deal and had much experience. However, your own personality always plays a crucial role. Much comes from one's intuition, from one's own life experience, and from spiritual maturity. In many respects, every session goes completely differently. The regression guide must therefore devote their complete attention to it. A good regression therapist will, in every moment, do exactly what's needed, use exactly the right means, and give exactly the guidance that's best for this client at this stage. This demands a very high level of alertness, and also a loving readiness to keep retuning in to that particular person.

I have continued to hear negative things from clients about how various regression guides have treated them. For example, some have tried to bring their religion or worldview into the session. Others have moralized or been judgmental. Still others were inattentive, brewing coffee during the session, filing their nails, or reading a magazine—things that have absolutely nothing to do with a good regression procedure.

One client was quite surprised when I told her that I would take as much time as I needed for the session even if it went over the previously arranged three hours. This was precisely because she had been with a regression therapist before who had concluded the session as soon as the agreed-upon time

had passed. This regression guide had paid absolutely no attention to which phase the regression was in and above all to what
condition the client found herself in, and indeed she was in a
condition where she needed attention and help. I was amazed
at the courage of this client for giving herself up once more
for a regression, although this one—as luck would have it—
came to a satisfactory conclusion.

Even if, with such a careless way of working, the consequences aren't quite so drastic, the client's trust is at the very
least mistreated and their openness abused. Unfortunately,
things like this happen in every profession, and it's definitely
not limited to the field of regression or to therapy in general.

If you want to look at things using the general law of attraction, you could say that everyone gets the therapist they
need in that moment. A bad therapist carries full responsibility for what they do and does not deserve any recognition.
However, they can ultimately bring about something good
completely unconsciously and even by mistake.

Several years ago, I was in communication with a garden-
er in Italy who told me that he had been deeply depressed
in the past, so he went to see a psychiatrist. She didn't treat
him in anything even resembling a humane way. She told him
to strip off his top half and she drew a feather all along his
back. After that she wrote him a prescription for some powerful psychiatric medication and sent him on his way. The
man went home and felt even more depressed, until his anger
kicked in. Why had he needed someone to make fun of him
this way? From now on he would take care of his own affairs!
"I tore up the prescription and then took my life into my own
hands, and it's become very nice indeed!" he said with a broad
grin on his face.

A Word on Regression CDs and Group Regressions

There are CDs offered in which the regression guide tries to place the listener in a trance and send them off on a journey into a past life. As people's souls will remain under protection even in this setting, I consider something like this to be relatively harmless, provided the listener is in a healthy psychological state. This kind of thing should not be taken too seriously, but rather should be treated as a kind of gimmick.

Nevertheless, this has nothing to do with a spiritual regression consultation as described here in this book. No matter what happens, the CD will simply unfold as it was recorded, and it will not be possible to respond to individual needs.

In a group regression, it also isn't possible to give sufficient room to the personal process being undergone by an individual. Nevertheless, there are certain kinds of group regressions that can be a good preparation for an individualized regression session.

chapter twelve

The Soul's Journey

You should already be able to form a fairly complete picture of all that a spiritual regression session contains and the kinds of fascinating possibilities for spiritual development and healing it provides. I have repeatedly addressed how such an experience can us assurance that our lives are embedded in a more extensive web of meaning and in a greater totality full of love and compassion. In this chapter I want to discuss fully this dimension of the spiritual and all that pertains to the soul.

It is not easy and ultimately it is not possible to describe the spirit world and the soul's levels using words. Nevertheless, words illuminate a great deal.

Understanding Oneself
as Part of a Greater Unity

Overall, for that fragment of a soul that has incarnated on Earth as a human, it's a question of recognizing that everything, really everything, is in essence already available inside it. Ultimately everything emerges from the all-encompassing One, and therefore every particle also contains the whole. The more that someone can take this concept into their consciousness, the more the feeling of separateness and fragmentation will fade.

It is a major project to bring the knowledge of all these different associations into human consciousness, and all the souls that participate in this do so happily and of their own free will. Every person also willingly goes into a body and into those earthly experiences.

But it's almost as if it's a rule that we have to forget this right at the start of the project when we are on Earth; as a result, a great many beings have the sure feeling that they don't want to come back down here again. However, this is really just a sign that they haven't yet learned to connect consciously with their soul and remember a deeper truth.

An alarmingly large number of people submit to the idea that life on Earth is a form of punishment and that Earth is a form of hell. Yes, it can go pretty hellishly for us on Earth, but that does not have to be so! It's a question of discovering that every person has a luminous soul and it's the task of every human to bring this soul energy and his or her highest vision down to Earth.

Every soul is shaped out of light, peace, love, goodness, and wisdom, out of humor, joy, and creativity, like the complete Being in the spirit world. Therefore these qualities are also dormant in every person, regardless of whether they are outwardly expressed or are deeply hidden and only shine through from time to time. Nevertheless, they are there and a person is on Earth because of them, for this is exactly the basic mission for every incarnation: to bring the qualities of the soul down to the terrestrial levels.

A Protracted, Ongoing Learning Process

We are all on this planet because it gives us the fascinating opportunity to live in a material world under the conditions of our respective individual life plans. The circumstances can vary, but learning and the integration of new experiences will always be in the forefront. It raises these fundamental questions: How can I make the best of what I meet with? How do I learn to bring my soul qualities down to Earth in this particular body—with or despite the conditions I encounter?

Evolution takes place throughout this entire learning process, as every soul part undergoes further experiences in every life that allow the soul to grow and ripen. All these events are stored in the soul, as well as the knowledge and wisdom that are gleaned from them. As a human being, you can only partially fall back on the experiences that your soul has already had. At any given time, only what is useful to us in the context of that particular reincarnation is accessible to us while we are on Earth. Human consciousness can fall back on various things, but other things have to be developed and cultivated anew and every incarnation has to do its work under ever-changing conditions. On one occasion it might be an issue of physical skills, while another time intellectual skills will be a priority, or emotional matters might be pushed more into the forefront.

Freedom to Shape the Life You Want

Every life on Earth is prepared in advance in the spirit world. In this the soul will be supported by its spirit guide and often by several soul companions as well, its "soul group." There are almost always several possibilities for the kind of life that one can choose as the next one. That can depend on which experiences might already have been completed, what is still in the offing, and what the soul might be interested in. Maybe the soul has harmed someone else in a previous life and would like to balance this out again. The possibilities are endless; the soul and the spirit guide jointly choose the most appropriate option.

At that time they always establish several criteria for the upcoming life, which then can't be amended any further. These include the country and the historical currents when one comes down into the world; parents; the body and the brain, with certain characteristics and options; family background; skin color; important other souls that one will encounter as a human being; life missions and goals; as well as some other meaningful life circumstances, which have already been put into place across the time span of that being.

The person is quite free in the direct shaping of a life. As a soul, that person knows what they would like to experience and achieve; however, whether they actually manage to remember this consciously or unconsciously when they are a human being and how they implement it are not predetermined. This is the mission and the challenge for every human life. Over the span of our life, our personal spirit guide stands by our side to help us.

"There's always someone who wants something from me. I never get any peace and quiet. I rush from appointment to appointment, and it's always me who has the responsibility. I am just overwhelmed. Just for once I would like to have nothing to do," complained a forty-year-old client of mine before a regression. Then he received a terribly boring past life in which nothing happened. Nothing. He was a man living near the end of the nineteenth century who had already received an inheritance from an aunt when he was fourteen, so he wasn't required to worry about getting an education or a job. Consequently, he just sat around. He got married, but his wife ran off after six months. It didn't seem to worry the man a whole lot; from then on he didn't do much, got bored, and died in his late fifties. The client complained, once back in the spirit world, about having to watch such a lame past life. His spirit guide passed a look to him and he understood the message behind it: be happy today that there are other people tugging at your sleeve and forcing you to do things, because if they didn't, you would let another life pass you by without meaning.

The blows of fate can also be valuable indications whenever a person has ignored the subtler signs they have been given. For example, a stressed person with a hectic life might initially have been given an easier way of integrating the theme of "quietness" into their life, such as a course in meditation that they've had in mind for a long time. However, they just never take the time for it. Eventually they come down with an illness that forces them to lie down at last and take things easy for a while. Seen like this, fate has been nothing more or less than a help for them in fulfilling their life plan.

It is one of the laws of this earth that we as humans here lose our memory of our soul consciousness right at the start of life. I don't think the veil of oblivion descends right at the moment of birth; many children know quite a bit in their first years of life about where they come from. It's not a rare occurrence, for example, to find them having a conversation with their spirit guide, their guardian angel, or however this being appears to them. Then forgetfulness sets in, bit by bit. There are only very few people for whom this does not happen; most of us, however, must live with forgetting.

This forgetting also has nothing to do with children having their wisdom driven out by their parents, the wider social surroundings, or society in general. Of course during this time children unfortunately do very often have the experience of not being understood or even of being laughed at when they communicate with a being from the spirit world that others simply can't perceive. This, however, is not the real reason for their forgetfulness. Forgetting is part of incarnation so that the soul will prove its worth every time, and it will see with relatively inexperienced eyes what there is on Earth to see. It will also start to remember more and more and gradually bring its life into harmony with the spirit world.

We need have no qualms about taking an unauthorized look behind the scenes when we undergo a regression. Those people for whom a regression is not appropriate will simply never even have the idea of wanting to do a session, or external circumstances will prevent it, or they will just not experience anything if they do it. The spirit world reveals to each person only what is appropriate and useful in terms of their evolution.

Always a New Chance

To souls looking out from the spirit world, an upcoming life on Earth seems like a wonderful and exciting game. While we are on Earth, life naturally feels much more serious most of the time. However, there is always a higher knowledge within us and there are always signs pointing out how we can do things better and how we can continue on our way with less pain and suffering and more joy and ease.

Often many things go wrong on Earth: a person doesn't bother with their previously determined lessons, doesn't take seriously the chances that crop up, is unhappy and doesn't pick up on the qualities that make up the soul's essence, and so on. Regardless of the problems that a person has gotten themselves entangled in, as long as that person still has life, they will still get another chance. Then perhaps if plan A doesn't work out, there is still plan B, plan C, and so on. A person can always correct, improve, or learn something, even if they can't do as much or do it as easily as they could at the start of the journey.

Ultimately it's all about giving your best step by step and day by day. Sometimes you only know what the right choice really was once the experience has been completed, or perhaps later on after death, when you are back in the spirit world. Serious errors only happen if you lose contact with your inner voice or soul.

One client experienced himself as a cruel and tyrannical ruler in Southeast Asia. He was stabbed to death at an early age, but he wasn't willing to accept that he was dead. In the midst of his power trip, he continued to rage, but it was an unpleasant experience for him because no one took any notice of his orders and his threats anymore. When he finally accepted that he was dead and arrived in the spirit world, he was rather embarrassed. As a soul, he knew that rulership in its truest and most noble sense was not a matter of intimidation but rather of service. That would have been his great challenge and his mission in life.

The more sincerely a person works on their personality growth, the more they will succeed in uncovering and expressing their own soul's qualities. They will learn how to get to know themselves as an inspired being and understand not only that they have a soul, but that they also are a soul.

This will lead to lasting change in their life. The person will be more content and will feel happier and yet more quiet and serene on the inside. Lessons will be gentler, and more pleasant experiences will be waiting on the road ahead. There will be more clarity in the person's life, more joy and self-possession. The feeling of grace, just to be on Earth and to be a self-incarnating soul, will move into the center of their consciousness. They will then come into contact more and more with the oneness of everything that is.

On the Road to Maturity

A human being with a broadly evolved soul leads a life full of joy and love. They live enthusiastically, enjoy learning, and are open to all the earthly experiences that might be delivered to them. They are inspired by a deep yearning to share this love and harmony with others too, as well as their inner knowledge, and to place all this helpfully at everyone's disposal. A more mature soul has compassion for itself and for others, for humans, animals, and nature. It has a higher vision, which it holds up as an example and which it tries to use for the benefit of all on Earth.

A long road spanning many incarnations might be needed to arrive at this level of soul maturity. In my experience with more than 4,000 spiritual regression clients, it has become clearer and clearer to me that the very first incarnations as a human being on Earth are sort of an intermediate stage, where a person is still very strongly connected to the spirit world, lives predominately in soul consciousness, and never completely forgets who they are, similar to what a child does. If you have already lived several incarnations on Earth, this knowledge of matters of the soul deteriorates over the course of the first few years. The more mature souls slowly remember it again much later. Most people are only conscious of it again for the first time after their death.

Different Points of View

You incarnate as both sexes. Some souls have a preference for a particular gender, but they all experience themselves within their reincarnation cycle as both a woman and a man. It is often the case that we will live our lives for a prolonged period of time as one gender and later as the other gender so that we can practice intensively what it means to be a man or a woman.

In my experience, it becomes steadily less important what gender we are across the course of our lives. In a certain sense we are all androgynous. Of course it does make a difference whether you are a man or a woman, whether you can beget children or actually give birth to them, as well as many other things. However, I don't perceive the apparently irreconcilable differences and the mutual incomprehension between the two sexes. We are not as different as we often believe we are. I consider it nonsense that men can't understand women and vice versa. Both genders are contained within each one of us, and most people already have lives as men and as women behind them. When we get away a bit from the superficial and go somewhat deeper, we can understand the other sex very well and in a certain sense put ourselves in their place. In this respect the role models in our society, with all its prejudices, are probably the most powerful influencing factors. However, these have no meaning in the soul dimensions.

I have regressed many clients from very strict cultural and religious backgrounds, and there's one thing that I can say for sure: as souls we are all equal in terms of our origins and our evolutionary path, and those divisive and judgmental differences that we hold to so strongly on Earth exist nowhere else.

Religion can be a good way to connect to one's spirituality if it is not dogmatic and it has as its goal connecting people with the spirit world and with their souls. When it helps people bring these qualities into terrestrial life, it can act like a vehicle that can bring us to our destination. There are different types of vehicles, and one should never mistake the means of travel for the actual destination and never worry which might be the one, single, correct vehicle. On the other hand, each one of us can only experience and deepen our spirituality on an inner level ourselves.

Whatever cultural background and social class a person comes from, and whatever the religion they belong to, in the spirit world that person identifies as a divine soul, experiencing beauty, love, compassion, and sharing as part of a light-filled cosmic whole. All that is complicated and divisive, which we like to cultivate and spread here on Earth, doesn't exist there. It turns out to be an illusion and it just dissolves.

One client's beloved only child died, and he had the feeling that now his love was dead. He felt empty and flat inside. During his regression, when he experienced his existence as a soul in the spiritual world, he could feel that his love was still there. In his grief he had closed himself off from it, but now he was able to bring it back. It became clear to him that he needed to send that love out to the rest of the world: to every person, every bird, every tree, every project. Then he would feel alive again and would reconnect with his life mission. He learned to recover from a heavy blow of fate, and in this way the death of his child wasn't meaningless for him anymore.

The external circumstances of life play a more modest role than we often assume. Whether someone spends their childhood in a war zone or in a time of peace, whether they have loving or cruel parents, whether they are healthy or infirm, rich or poor—all that says nothing about what sort of character they have, their progress in their spiritual evolution, and what the person will learn over their life's course. A person might even realize later that it was most helpful to have grown up in difficult circumstances.

A rich and sheltered daughter might find it a lot harder to gain access to the deeper meaning of life because she doesn't feel any great compulsion to change anything about her life. A person who is completely despondent because of horrible external circumstances could feel the burning conviction inside that there has to be something else out there. This person will search, and will do so with such power and diligence that they will perhaps come up with something very quickly.

From a spiritual perspective, being human means being able to live out your soul qualities through the medium of a physical body, regardless of the exterior circumstances and conditions. Every one of us is granted as much as we need to be able to create our desired experiences and reach our highest goals.

One person might have a particularly keen intelligence and should learn to use it for the benefit of all. Another might instead seem somewhat dim, but that could be for the purposes of learning to be unconditionally happy from the heart about the smaller things in life. Perhaps this person was very intelligent in a previous life, but was at the same time a lonely and dissatisfied eccentric, and now they are experiencing the opposite. They had wanted to have a less demanding brain for once, for the purpose of finding more gratitude and joie de vivre.

Maybe someone else was an utter villain who had murdered, raped, and stolen, and now they have incarnated into a set of conditions where the probability is great that they will experience the same things being done to their own physical body. This may allow their soul to develop some human compassion out of their own direct personal experience of suffering. There are probably very malicious people who keep experiencing moments of clarity in which they can see briefly that what they have done is horrible, yet they keep on forgetting this every time. As a soul, they know they didn't manage to empathize with other people to a sufficient extent in that past life, but now they can experience for themselves the suffering of this heavy fate, and in this way they will mature.

Perhaps another person, for whom in a previous life nothing ever seemed good enough, will also find out through their poverty-stricken circumstances how it feels to be grateful for a simple meal or to have a roof over their head. They will come to understand for themselves that they can't make any assumptions about life, and this realization will bring them satisfaction.

The People Who Accompany Us

We will often know people from a previous life who are important for us today. We frequently incarnate together with members of our soul group. That's the name we use for souls who are close to us in the spirit world, who are about as far along the path of soul evolution as we are, and who have learned with us. When we meet one on Earth, we can support each other and remind each another directly or indirectly about our life missions. A person from one's soul group will often seem remarkably familiar on first meeting. These beings who are closely related on a soul level can be blood relatives, but often they are close friends and life partners. They don't always have to be people we love during our time on Earth. They can even be the people who irritate us and who we have the greatest difficulties with. Ultimately they will always drive us toward our further evolution.

Sometimes these soul relatives are people we have business with for only a short time. This can be a teacher who taught someone a specialized subject between the ages of eight and ten, but who thus created a turning point and awoke something in the child that becomes important for the rest of their life. If this person, now aged forty, wonders who their soul relatives might be, this teacher probably would not come to mind initially. Instead the person might be more likely think of a new partner in relationship that seems spiritual to an extent but really isn't special.

The different constellations in which the souls from one group can meet each other again on Earth are quite varied. Individual roles can change: once as best friend, once as beloved, once as a competitor, and once as grandmother. Sometimes a soul can also incarnate completely without companion souls so that it can find out how it feels to be in the world without these intimate friends and to have to turn to other people more often. There could be a different task of learning to make contact with your soul group through dreams and inward experiences.

Some souls make quite specific arrangements for the upcoming life to include others who don't belong to their soul group. Five souls might get together because at a certain time they want to build a hospital together. It is planned that one of them, who's been most involved in the project already, will manage its administration. One will look after the healthy nutrition of the patients, another will cover people's preventative care, a third will be the chief medical officer, and finally another will act as the interior designer. Whether and how all these things take place is not predetermined. The appointment, however, remains.

If someone who had been one of the original participants dies prematurely through a drug overdose, then that person won't be able to keep the date; the individual will not be present for the realization of this hospital project. Perhaps some of the other participants believed that this person was weak, incapable, and not much use for anything—including the hospital project. Perhaps these people even know each other, or perhaps they only notice it in due course, but ultimately they arrive at the conclusion that this person will not be part of the project. The other four could get on with the project alone. Perhaps another person chances upon them, someone who wasn't part of the original arrangement but who fits in with the conditions for the realization of the project. Of course there is always the chance that the whole thing won't actually come together because for too many of them their lives have gone in a different direction from the one planned in the spirit world, and consequently the whole arrangement can't be coordinated.

The souls who originally made the appointment then meet again after death, and those who failed to keep to the plan are confronted: Why didn't you come? Why didn't you keep to our arrangement? Together they look at which particular decisions and actions in the life just past got in the way of the arrangement. Then the souls can process it and learn from it.

An Appointment with the Love of Your Life?

There are many different forms of arrangements. Perhaps there are souls who know whom they want to marry and who will be their children. Even for those people who make an advance arrangement for a loving relationship, things can unfold quite differently when they are actually on Earth.

It's pretty certain that the two people will meet, but whether the relationship will then really be entered into and become a wonderful thing is not set in stone. They will perhaps have to overcome many obstacles so that they can first learn and grow. Sometimes those obstacles end up being so difficult that one or both of them don't want to take on the relationship. They separate, get divorced, and then destroy the mutual happiness that would have been possible.

Perhaps they poison each other's lives instead of mutually supporting each other with love and respect. One might have been able to publish books, while the other could have learned an alternative healing method and then practiced it. However, with all their arguing, there was no energy left to pursue these options. Sure, there are also many learning experiences hidden in a great love that has gone sour, but the pain wasn't really necessary and it could have gone more smoothly, easily, and joyfully.

Sometimes it is also the case that a great love or friendship is only meant to exist for a certain length of time, and it is appropriate for them then to part again. Even if a marriage disintegrates after many years because the partners involved notice that their life paths have to develop in different directions, that doesn't mean that the two of them don't still love each other or that they were wrong for each other. There simply could have been important experiences that they could not have undergone with each other. It might have been the experience of loneliness that could have followed or the experience of entering into a loving relationship again and with other people. From the perspective of the soul, there is no moralizing and no value judgment in this context.

Many people wonder whether they will see those whom they were close to in life after death. This can be affirmed with absolute confidence: in every case you will meet the people and animals you loved once again in the spirit world.

Karma

When we speak of souls coming back again and again to Earth in order to experience something, learn something, or compensate for some debt in the past, there's a Sanskrit word that leaps quickly to mind: karma. If we asked a Buddhist to give us a picture of their teaching on reincarnation, they would say that a human being must be reborn for as long as it takes for their karma to be dissolved. In the Christianity-dominated West, we would probably conclude from this that life on Earth is therefore a form of punishment, but that's not what is meant. It would be helpful from our point of view to shed some light on this matter.

Even if it's the soul's aim to go back into the condition of non-separation and into the cosmic totality, the way there—every step and every day of life on Earth—can and should be marked by compassion and joy. Ultimately the whole "making your way back to the One" is only an illusion, for nothing is ever separate from anything else and nothing can ever fall away from the One. It's not a question of attaining the One, but of rediscovering it and making yourself aware that we are all connected to everything, in the same way it is not a question of becoming a soul but of remembering that you are a soul.

The term "karma" is often misunderstood. Many people assume that it is a kind of penalty for earlier unjust actions. However, punishments only exist on the level of human existence and are also there to fulfill a purpose. On the other hand, on the spiritual level there is only repentance for all the other wrongs that have been committed, as well as the deep desire to bring luminosity to the earth, to heal all that is dark and to lift it up to the light.

Basically karma is nothing else but effect—the effect that results from an imbalance between polarities. It marks the sum of everything that someone has experienced and done, for good as well as evil.

As long as someone has intentionally injured another life, they haven't realized what life means. But as long as they let themselves be hurt, they still don't understand it. Here also the affected person is held captive by suffering and by their belief in it.

For a time (and this can stretch out over a large number of lives) things always go back and forth: one time a person lives more as a victim, then as more of a perpetrator, then as a victim all over again, and in the following life back as a perpetrator—for as long as the person identifies with one pole and tries to avoid the other one. At some point we become aware of both sides, and we realize that they are actually interdependent. This is how they pass through our attention into our life: a person wants to have one pole and not the other. So we all give energy to both manifestations of the poles.

One client's theme was always envy, whether she was experiencing it herself or was being envied by others. She experienced herself in a particular past life as a woman who killed her brother out of envy. When she met up with him again in the spirit world and was made aware of what she had done, she swore once and for all to stop comparing herself with others. That was where her dissatisfaction and envy sprang from. She wanted instead to be happy for herself and others. By recalling this experience, she was finally able to leave the theme of envy behind her, in this current life.

With a steadily growing awareness, a person then becomes the director of their life. They drift less and less often into those victim/perpetrator roles and live instead out of joy, out of love for others, and out of the awareness that everything is connected. This sense of being good arises from living our life in resonance with our own inner truth. It doesn't come from striving to be good so that later we don't end up in hell. It also doesn't happen because we hope to get this or that out of it or we fear that otherwise other people might not like us anymore.

Incidentally there is no hell that you are sent to after death. There are hellish conditions on Earth and there is the great regret that the soul feels when it has committed evil acts as a human being. The soul can feel how badly it has injured itself when it has harmed others, be they humans, animals, plants, or the earth itself. Even if the soul knows that some benefit or learning will result, it still feels an undeniable need to make amends. It knows that it must once again settle the negative karma that has accumulated through this unkind action. It does not do so, however, out of a fear of punishment, but instead out of a deep empathy for the victims and the desire to put everything back into order. When the soul resolves to work on this in a future life, it should do so out of love and a positive affirmation of life and without sadness or a sense of guilt, because otherwise it would create more negative karma.

Attaching ourselves to beautiful things also produces karma. It's good to be free from attachments to outward manifestations and to trust joyfully in the flow of life.

chapter thirteen

Cycles of Rebirth

From a human point of view, there is much that is barely comprehensible about the spiritual dimension. For example, the soul doesn't share our concept of time, the notion of chronology in which we always continue to evolve. As we can experience, for example, in deep meditation, there is no time there anymore and also no separation between ourselves and what is ostensibly outside us. Time on the soul level can be compared with the unfolding water lily, which opens simultaneously in every direction.

On Earth, and in the human cognizance, those things of course do exist—they are "reality" in our everyday consciousness. In a certain sense the cycle of rebirth—which every incarnated soul on Earth lives through—can also be conceived of with respect to time. How far a soul advances in its evolution can vary a lot. Some souls proceed as far as the highest possible perfection, and others end their cycle on Earth relatively early because the experiences they had and what they wanted to learn from them were sufficient.

It varies a great deal how long a soul stays in the spirit world until its next reincarnation. Some souls want to go back to Earth as quickly as possible, while others remain longer in the spirit world.

Many souls already have countless incarnations behind them. Every soul has its own evolution speed. Some souls are highly industrious and advance very quickly through relatively few Earth lives and manage to integrate a rich store of experiences. Others need a lot longer; they give themselves more time and learn very little across many incarnations.

The Cycle of Reincarnation Reaches Its End

Sometimes there are souls who have finished their incarnation cycle and go back to Earth because they are collaborating on a project that hasn't quite been completed, or are there to help other souls realize their potential by acting as their spiritual teacher or healer.

The more a person connects with and understands their identity as a soul, the more compassionate and loving they are toward their fellow creatures. The intentional or even thoughtless torture or killing of other beings or the passive acquiescence of such actions becomes impossible to them, as they feel love, understanding, and responsibility for everything. They recognize more and more the divine in all that is. They come closer to oneness, and in them grows a deep desire to help end ignorance and bring appreciation, light, and all-encompassing divine love to Earth. All this manifests out of a feeling of exultant joy and deep gratitude. Such a person loves life and consciously brings their soul qualities down to Earth.

From there the reincarnation cycle approaches its end and the wheel of rebirth comes gradually to a standstill. This person has become the soul that they actually already were.

Animals as Our Fellow Creatures

There is a great deal more to say than is possible within the scope of this book about the soul dimension of animals, the differences between humans and other animals, and the tasks that animals have on this earth. However, there are a few things that should be included that will help us understand the interdependency between them.

Obviously animals also have souls, and after death they likewise arrive in the spirit world. Sometimes the souls of animals are so hurt by what the people on Earth did to them that initially they don't need anything but healing. Just like humans after death, they make their way to specific spheres in the spirit world to regenerate themselves.

Animals go through a different kind of reincarnation cycle: they always remain innocent and connected to their soul awareness. An exception to this could be certain primates, which partly retain certain human aspects.

Animals always live in the present moment and their thoughts don't stray into the past or the future. If you leave them just to be animals, they live exactly the way that they were made to. It's the same with a flower: it just blooms. It makes the best of what it is and doesn't question whether it would be better off as a tree or even as another flower. It doesn't mull over whether it is doing things right or whether it is worthy or whether it deserves to bloom. These are human questions that have no relevance to plants or animals.

So just as humans always incarnate as humans, so animals always come to the earth as animals. I am aware of only a very few cases where a human soul has on one occasion made an excursion into the animal kingdom. Animals often remain in the same form, although it is also possible for them to gather experiences living as a different species.

After their death on Earth, animal souls decide whether they want to come back to Earth. A species extinction can occur when certain animals don't want to incarnate in one particular form any more or don't even want to incarnate at all. That we choose to make external conditions responsible for this—which can be man-made or also natural climactic changes—is not wrong from a soul perspective: external conditions always set the yardstick for which physical forms are still feasible on Earth. At the same time also the desire of souls to experience something specific will also shape the environment. So the conditions are created in which they can incarnate with all their particular projects.

Humans and animals have different areas of responsibility. A significant difference between the two is that a person can consciously choose. We have the freedom to decide, and with it we also carry the responsibility for everything that we think, say, and do. It's different for an animal, which is restricted in terms of the choices it can make and lives the path that nature has selected for it.

A woman who had great difficulty showing love to her children experienced herself in a past life as a lad of around sixteen. When he was only just seven, his parents gave him away to work for the lord of the manor and he worked as a stable boy. This very withdrawn young man, who had always been emotionally neglected by other people, learned what was meant by affection, tenderness, attention, and love from the horses he cared for and with whom he also slept at night. The horses were his friends and his family, and he felt wonderfully protected and accepted by them. So it was important for my client now to find these good feelings in herself and in her present life and to pass them on to her children.

Animals do not have the kind of intelligence that we have, and they don't need it. They do, however, have a level of perception and abilities in many other areas that we, to a great extent, don't even suspect exist and in which they are frequently vastly superior to us.

Animals form an essential part of the act of creation. You could say that the divine has split itself up into anything you might conceive of, including rocks, plants, animals, etc., and people. Everything that lives on Earth maintains a perfectly balanced equilibrium. Thus animals, in their thousands upon thousands of different manifestations—from the tiniest insects to the largest mammals—are also the stabilizers of this natural balance, while meanwhile they are taking their own steps in learning and in evolution. Without human beings, this balance on Earth would never be jeopardized. On the contrary: this balance would be safeguarded for a much longer period of time without humanity's aggressive interventions. No earthly harmony is imaginable, however, without the animal world; if an individual species dies out in a particular area, we sometimes then get a hint of how much everything has to be rearranged anew.

Everything created has its own specific task, and it falls of course to humanity to respect and maintain that delicate balance on Earth. However, this doesn't happen very often. Animals and nature are abused and exploited on a large scale. When we use the biblical phrase "subdue the earth" as permission for this, this is evidence of a major misunderstanding and not least the spiritual indolence and emotional callousness of certain people. For whoever explores this phrase more deeply and listens then to their heart has to come to a very different interpretation: only humans can freely choose their thoughts and behavior. With this tremendous freedom comes the responsibility to use it for the good of the whole and thus also for the good of every individual being. This is the only sense in which human beings subdue the earth: by learning to subdue themselves. So a true ruler is never a tyrant and an exploiter, but serves the kingdom using the best of their knowledge and conscience.

Since everything ultimately is one, you can't really pose the question of relative value. That would almost be as grotesque as the question of whether a leg is worth more than an arm.

Learning from Animals

Most people have forgotten who they really are and what their tasks are in the earthly dimension. That's no excuse, though, not to keep evolving, because each person has every opportunity to remember this at every step. It is also their mission to do this. The animals are here as well to help us do this: an animal can be a wonderful teacher to us, not least because of their ability to remain in the present moment—an attribute that is always required for achieving enlightenment. As it says in the Bible, "become as little children." This is a road to evolution. This refers to innocence in the way that small children radiate it and animals likewise set us an example. An animal lives as its species dictates. It is never brutal or vicious, even when it is eating another animal. It lives out its animal agenda and enjoys it. It would never consider how it could harm another being—that's something that only a perverted human brain could consider.

Animals also teach us about compassion and charity. The fact that animals come to Earth to live alongside humans is an act of kindness. They often carry a heavy load and ultimately remind us what love, forgiveness, trust, humility, and being in the now really mean. For those who look closely, animals can be the greatest teachers. They live according to their nature in a state of union with the spirit world—just like we should do.

One client of mine lived a past life as a solitary woman who hadn't felt any happiness since the death of her sister, with whom she had lived for decades. She was nearly ninety years old and complained all the time that no one took care of her emotionally. She was greeted in the spirit world by her spirit guide, who had a special surprise for her: her cat. Now, as a soul, the woman realized that this animal had wanted to be her friend and confidant on Earth and that she could have had a lot of fun with it. Full of shame, she had to admit that she had certainly never recognized her cat as an aware being. She had always chased it away and even insulted it and given it an occasional kick.

That we human beings initially lose our soul awareness and must rediscover it after a long period of evolution is one of the specified conditions of our incarnation. As long as we don't know who we really are, we slip into all kinds of comfortable roles. We tend to put on a show for others and for ourselves, and thus more than anything else we feed our ego. On the other hand, animals don't play any roles; they are authentic in an unconditional way, which is something that we have to learn all over again. An animal also doesn't try to be better than others; it doesn't need anything else other than to live out its own identity. It is in harmony with itself. All the negative human qualities and behavior patterns that can be found wherever a person hasn't yet discovered the connection with their soul are foreign to animals.

Many of my clients love animals and often feel much more comfortable in their company than they do with people. With animals, they have the feeling of being warmly accepted. On the other hand, with people, they have the feeling of having to protect themselves from emotional injury. I think that we will have made an immensely great evolutionary stride forward if we behave in such a way that we can respectfully interact with all our fellow humans, every animal, and the whole of nature and when we can all cohabitate free from anxiety and in harmonious accord.

Some animals keep returning to Earth with certain people. For example, I have worked with a man who came to Earth several times accompanied by an animal. The two of them formed a wonderful team across many lives, were of great help to each another, and taught each other significant things.

Only pets incarnate intentionally within the orbit of certain people and then are very tightly bound to their respective families. Thus they assume many of their problems, cares, and even illnesses. They bear these difficulties for their humans, so they often get utterly overwhelmed and abused.

One client's most important confidant was her dog. She was worried, though, because he was getting increasingly nervous and sometimes aggressive as well. In a past life she saw herself as a poor cowherd in the sixteenth century, and these animals were her best friends. On the basis of the relationship between this cowherd and the cows out in the open air, the woman realized that today she engaged far too little with the needs of her dog and—although she loved him—she went outdoors with him and let him run around far too rarely. She also recognized that he functioned inappropriately as a kind of relationship substitute for her. She placed a lot of human demands on him. It became clear to her that a pet is always there for people according to its particular capabilities, but that an animal also has needs, which definitely have to be fulfilled.

Vets who work holistically know that the symptoms of an unwell animal often allow conclusions to be made about the health and inner state of their owner. It's part of our responsibility as human beings to meet the innocence, love, and care that animals bring to us with respect, gratitude, and just as much care and love.

I really don't need to elaborate any further on the enormous failings that still exist in this area. Even allegedly well-intentioned practices, such as animal testing in the pharmaceutical industry, for example, or in branches of cosmetics that are ostensibly carried out to protect the consumer are no excuse for cruelty. The same and even better results can and should be reached without animal cruelty, as many studies and firms and their products have proved today. Every single person is responsible for everything that happens on Earth and can rethink their position on any matter and improve their behavior. So it's not unimportant whether we buy the products of industrial mass animal farming or of humane animal welfare. There are many cleaning products and cosmetics available that have not been tested on animals, and organic farming and the goods that come from it are most definitely better for the ecological balance of nature and also healthier for us.

One client of mine was already more than seventy when she relived a past life with me where she lived happily with animals. After the session, for the first time in her life she stroked the soft coat of a dog, which caused it to wag its tail joyfully. In her surprise she declared: "That never used to happen! I didn't get a skin rash or feel out of breath. It's just wonderful!" In her childhood it had been deeply instilled in her that animals were disgusting and dirty, so she had not been able to come into contact with them. What a thing to deny yourself your whole life!

I would like to use a personal experience to demonstrate that this part of our lives is not a sideshow but is a core concern both for the individual soul and the spirit world. One of my clients was in the spirit world and felt himself suddenly deflected off the true path he was currently working on. He went with great hesitancy and only with the support of his spirit guide into a gloomy tower. Inside, all sorts of animal corpses were stacked up. They'd been horribly treated; many were skinned and others dismembered. I asked the client what these images might be saying to him. His answer then surprised me greatly: "This is a message for you, actually! My spirit guide says it's very important that you stand up for animal protection. You must continue to do this. Write about it in your book!" This client knew nothing before the session about the initiatives in this area that I had already begun!

The Question of Guilt

We all come to Earth with a definite mission. There's a lot for each one of us that we haven't yet discovered and that we'd really like to experience. Maybe we want to prove ourselves in some way or experience something firsthand that we have only gone through previously from the opposite perspective. Some might say reproachfully, "But it can't be the case that someone would choose of their own free will to go through a bad experience!" When we discuss this, we can arrive pretty quickly in the territory of perpetrator and victim, of guilt and innocence, of the whole debate around forgiveness and responsibility. It is a delicate issue, but one that should be discussed openly.

Victims and Perpetrators

The first point I would like to make in this regard is that there is no excuse for those who knowingly do horrible things to others, be they humans, animals, plants, or the environment. In my experience, it's not the case that a soul might say: "I want you to kill me—thanks! And because I wanted it, that leaves you free of blame, because I just had to experience it." That's definitely not how it goes. These types of interpretations only result in misleading theories. Such an attempt to excuse all the dreadful stuff that affects people all the time is bound to fail.

What might seem strange at first to many people, in the context of our modern daily life and our materialistic way of thinking, is the fact that everything that happens to a person has something to do with them on an inner level. Even if bad things happen, it's not through pure chance that we experience them. Victim and perpetrator have an affinity with each other. This, however, has nothing to do with blame, as we might view it from an earthly perspective. This is the Law of Attraction at work. The thoughts, beliefs, and feelings of the victim, in this life and in a previous life, have made possible the actions of the perpetrator. In a certain sense the perpetrator is "only" the vehicle. However, that doesn't stop the person from being responsible for their actions.

Victim and perpetrator encounter one another on the same level, just so they can make the event happen. They are mutually dependent. Most of the time the victim was once the perpetrator and vice versa. This pattern can repeat itself endlessly. You could say that both of them, victim and perpetrator, have not yet managed to extricate themselves from the cycle of polarity.

Ultimately it becomes a question of we humans not being the perpetrator nor the victim, but of becoming the free creators of our existence. Until then it is a bit like a game of table tennis: perpetrator, victim, perpetrator, victim—and so it goes on.

Almost every soul has a life behind them that they can barely bring themselves to face. Anyone who has spent a period of time on Earth usually cannot avoid counting themselves among life's murderers, schemer, and thieves. It's certainly not something that is intentional and without doubt it could go differently; however, it's all part of the freedom humans have to make the wrong decision and fall a long way down.

Even if everyone could come up with some reason or other for their unpleasant behavior, it lies within our responsibilities as human beings to sort out our own injuries and aggressive compulsions so that no one else is blamed for them. You can't just say, "I had to act like that because so much was done to me." That can't be put forward as an excuse.

Here is an interesting story that illuminates this concept. In his cell, a mass murderer was waiting to be executed. A journalist interviewed him and asked why he had done so many terrible things. The murderer answered: "I had absolutely no choice. I come from a poor family. My father was a violent man who mistreated and beat my mother, and I had to watch that happen every day. It was terrible. I couldn't have ended up anything other than violent myself." Now this man had a twin brother who worked in a small community as a helpful, caring pastor, beloved by all. The journalist tracked him down and asked him why he stood up so much for others. He answered: "I had absolutely no choice. I come from a poor family. My father was a violent man who mistreated and beat my mother, and I had to watch that happen every day. It was terrible. I couldn't have ended up doing anything but try to make things better, to develop compassion and be there for others."

Accepting the Role You Are Playing

How people deal with the undoubtedly difficult theme of perpetrator and victim varies when they see themselves in the very unattractive role of perpetrator in a regression. A murder, rape, act of torture, or other gruesome deed might take place—and they themselves, as that person in that past life, are the perpetrator. It requires great openness and inner strength to be able to take up this kind of role. It's often much easier for us to play out the role of victim. If you can experience life just once from the other side, you can learn to develop a greater understanding of yourself and others. Then the sincere desire to work on yourself and to bring your own light-filled soul down to humanity on Earth will also be strengthened.

In regressions, I find it significant that a violent, untruthful, and malicious person is never really happy. They may be materially successful and enjoy great power, but inside they lack calm, love, and peace.

In a past life, a little girl's parents were killed. She knew that their neighbor had done it, but could not prove it, and he never was caught. She managed later on, however, to lead a happy life as an adult. She knew inside that it wasn't up to her to shed any light on this deed or to avenge it. She then discovered in the spirit world that her approach had been correct. Her task was to enjoy life in spite of it all—the murderer would have to atone for his actions later and on another level. This had nothing to do with her.

Every soul's essence is full of love and light. It's rare to encounter souls that have damaged themselves through terrible deeds across a great many incarnations to the extent that they require help and need to be transformed by other souls. When this is the case, these souls stay for a long time in special secluded locations until they are healed. Only then are they allowed to incarnate again.

The solution, during the time before and after death, isn't to beat yourself up for a bad deed or to become morose, shut-down, or embittered. That won't help anyone. The best strategy is to perceive your own deed clearly, repent honestly, forgive yourself and others, try to learn from it, and, if possible, make amends and do a better job in the future—immediately today or, if one is already dead, in the next life.

If, for example, a person has stolen something from someone, the person can apologize for their behavior—but then the issue still hasn't been settled. Only once the stolen object has been given back is the incident truly resolved. A person is held responsible for their actions, however far back in the past it might go, until the deed has been balanced out.

chapter fourteen

Dos and Don'ts of Spiritual Development

A great many people—often those who like to judge others harshly—consider themselves to be good people. Sometimes you can see how a dark side comes to the fore with such people when they attain a certain level of power. Even here in our Western Christian culture, we have a decidedly twisted image of so-called good people. Acting outwardly upright, inconspicuous, and as joyless as possible has got very little to do with what we are as souls.

People who are mature on the soul level, and at peace with themselves, can't and won't do anything other than act in the world out of charity and joy. It would curtail their quality of life to experience others as unhappy without making any attempt to help them. Otherwise they themselves would end up unhappy too.

Dos and don'ts of spiritual development are initially very important. However, once you start to make some progress in your personal development, you will no longer cause harm to anyone and you will want to work for the greater good. And at a certain point you will feel that you are hurting yourself if you "just" kill a fly or squash a spider.

From a broader perspective, there is also the balance between the different sides: if someone as a man has oppressed women, then perhaps in a later incarnation he himself might experience life as an oppressed woman. That has nothing to do with retribution; it's a matter of deeper learning—of experiencing, as it were, the other side of the coin. From that point on, this soul will know a lot more about the topic and will be capable of more love and understanding, something it couldn't do before this life.

A client experienced a past life as a woman who had been raped. After death, the perpetrator met the client as a soul in heaven and asked for forgiveness. The soul was able to forgive and also recognized that it had learned a great deal from this terrible experience for the life that was to follow. The client, in his life today, showed great respect to his wife and both his daughters. He expressed his sexual side in a very loving way and without any desire for power. He realized that to a large extent all this was connected to the horrible experience from the past and that this then had not been in vain. The client went through a deeply moving session that gave him a profound sense of the meaning of all that had happened in his life.

The fact that everything is linked in karma, reincarnation, and the higher will as a soul does not, however, give a person carte blanche to behave maliciously. There is wise and timeless guidance for us to discover in the saying "Do unto others what you would have them do unto you."

When a person is making their way step by step into soul consciousness, they will get caught up less often in the polarity between victim and perpetrator. They will stop causing harm to others and will also, where possible, not get hurt themselves anymore. With increasing maturity, the person will gain ever more trust in life, see the divine in others, and protect themselves from the things that might cause harm.

There are always two sides to consider. As a human being I can get very angry with someone who has done something to me or to another. However, on the soul level I can also feel love for them and recognize them as a being whose core is illuminated but who has gotten mixed up and has inflicted pain on others and ultimately on the self. One can and should defend oneself both despite and with this love. This can even go so far as supplying a just and legal punishment to another person who has committed a great injustice.

Illness, Pain, and Misery

Our earthly existence is often overshadowed by all kinds of pain, illness, and misery. We have to endure many terrible things, and it can be pretty difficult to see any meaning in it. Our sympathy and practical support will often be in demand during the times when we ourselves are in a better situation. People can then grow beyond themselves and learn more about themselves in all-encompassing love and selfless service. This can be a great gift that can act like a catalyst to spiritual ripening.

Our ability to evaluate situations will quickly reach its limit if it is only in tune with the earthly dimensions of suffering. Each individual fate is embedded in a deeper one that has as its goal connecting people with their higher life plan. Often, though, it is only possible for us to recognize this later on, sometimes only after death. Through a spiritual regression we can sometimes recognize these kinds of connections a lot earlier and also with greater clarity.

When a person is ill on and off throughout their life, there can be various higher causes for this. Perhaps in earlier lives they were always a strong and physically oriented person, who now for the first time wants to experience how it feels for the body not to function well so that they can try to develop further mentally and emotionally.

Perhaps they also need to suffer a specific illness because they have made it a long-term goal to discover a cure for this affliction and consequently need the experience of what it's like to suffer from it themselves. Perhaps this soul was a doctor in a much earlier life, an herbal wisewoman in the one following, and then a nurse—and now finally it wants to experience the illness from the other side and find out what it's like to lie in a sick bed themselves and have to be looked after.

A client who was suffering from cancer saw herself in a past life as a woman who was healthy but who just didn't want to live anymore. Her husband had left her and the children had left home, so she sat outside in the cold, neglected herself, and stopped taking care of her body. She literally let herself die.

Her spirit guide clearly showed this client that she still had this tendency in her life today. It was up to her to decide either to let herself die prematurely or to engage constructively with her life. The woman realized that she had to keep going with the treatments she had started. She saw that she wanted to learn to experience fully everything the earth has to offer, even with those difficult challenges, which this time involved the vulnerabilities that exist on a more physical plane. Running away from it all because that seemed to be the simplest way? She didn't want to repeat that mistake.

People's creativity can grow across many lifetimes. Great inventions or significant changes in society, research, medicine, or the arts never happen overnight. It's more often the case that individual souls have prepared for it over a long period of time, and have collected knowledge in many areas and roles so they can then bring something completely new into the world based on this store of experiences.

There are so many options and so many reasons for a soul to select a particular life or destiny. I have become very careful with my interpretations and assessments of the outcomes during the many years in which I have experienced regressions on myself and on others. More often than not, I am amazed by the wisdom that comes out of our lives, even if we don't really perceive it ourselves in any deep way on a daily basis.

A very difficult issue is that of the suffering of innocent people—of children, for example. On the soul level, every being is in agreement with what happens; otherwise it just wouldn't happen. However, I must reiterate that these spiritual aspects do not absolve anyone of their guilt should they deliberately do something evil to another person. They bear total responsibility for their actions.

If, for example, a young child dies from an incurable disease, this is something that was prearranged in their life's plan. However, this need not involve guilt in any shape or form.

Even if it's very hard to understand, it can be thought of as an aid to the further evolution of those who are bereaved.

One of the worst things that can happen to you is when your own child dies. However, many people who have experienced this say that after a few years it can eventually feel like a kind of gift. Because of it they have changed their lives completely and have adopted an entirely different attitude about what life really is; everything now has a depth and an awareness that just wasn't there before.

For their part, the child will often say, as a soul once it has arrived after death in the spirit world, that it went to Earth to be a kind of teacher for the parents and that it took this early death upon itself so that they could learn from it. Sometimes the parents will still be grieving, even though the soul of the dead child is already back with them once again as a newborn baby.

Here one must make a very fine distinction. If, for example, someone dies from alcohol abuse or literally rots in front of the television, that most definitely wasn't preplanned. It was the poor decision of the single person involved, and they themselves have to answer for it accordingly.

In extreme situations, a person will start to pose increasingly essential questions. What's now happening on Earth? What are we human beings doing here? What could the true meaning of life on Earth be? What sort of project is this... the earth? Are there rules of the game, and who came up with them? How can they be implemented? Is there life after death?

After some extreme life events, some people can claim after death, "In the end, I asked the right questions and I worked some things out." Or they clearly see where their limitations lie—ones that they can't transcend—and this makes them more modest and humble. Perhaps someone will learn that things can happen that are so appalling that it's possible to leave your body. One female client told me during a regression: "I am being raped and mutilated, but I am not really there anymore. I have already left my body and am watching from outside. Otherwise I would go mad."

The Question of Proof

In a scientific sense, there is no proof that we go through past lives and are reborn. There is also no proof for the existence of the soul, spirit guides, and the spirit world. The reason for this is that the criteria for proof, as defined by science, have been set within a limited, scientifically oriented body of thought. Only that which can be authenticated using recognized testing methods is deemed to be proven. According to this way of thinking, nothing else is allowed to exist. With rational thinking alone, the spiritual dimensions are not attainable, but that's because of the restricted nature of human understanding. Naturally, our rational understanding gets overwhelmed by the whole subject of regression, but to that understanding it just doesn't exist in this narrow context.

One man started to doubt, after a session, whether what he had experienced in trance was actually true. He became so preoccupied with his thoughts that he really didn't pay any more attention to the important messages that the session had brought up for him to help him further his development. In the end, he asked the spirit world for a sign. The next day he was going into town and he saw a statue just like one that had been shown to him in his past life. He had never noticed this statue before in the town he'd been living in. This inscription was on the base of the statue: "Only doubt stands in the way of true knowledge."

There are and have been in the past many attempts to substantiate the events of an earlier life using historical facts. For example, people have traveled to the places where the events took place and tried to find confirmation of the evidence offered up by that past life. Or someone has searched the Internet or through history books about the period they experience firsthand in their session and made immense efforts to turn up any corroborating details.

In many television documentaries on this topic, I was blessed to be the regression expert, working with a team of distinguished historians and journalists. By use of dedicated hypnosis techniques, we were able to historically verify a surprising number of details from our clients' reports given in trance during regression. However, in daily life, typically only a small percentage of the information contained in the regression can be verified. To a great extent this is because it takes so much time and money to carry out such a comprehensive investigation. If the past life was too long ago, and the places have changed a lot or have disappeared completely, there are hardly going to be any clues to be found. It often happens that the client will mix up their current knowledge with their experiences from the past so that some of it will actually not be true. The main point, however, of a therapeutically oriented regression doesn't actually lie in verifiable facts.

We have probably all had the experience where we're thinking about somebody and then they phone us. We might arrive in a completely new neighborhood, yet somehow it seems familiar to us. Or we might meet a person for the first time and have the feeling we have known each other for eons. We all have a notion that there is that inexplicable something that transcends our understanding. We all have a great deal more access to such phenomena than we commonly believe. If a person doesn't want to admit this, they don't have to, but they shouldn't then pass judgment on other people's experiences in this area.

Spheres in Which No Proof Is Necessary

I remember a scientist asking me to use the power of my mind to influence some substance in a test tube. I had said once that I thought this was possible, and now he wanted me to take part in an experiment along those lines. At first I found it exciting, but then it occurred to me that this researcher would remain the same rational skeptic no matter how the experiment turned out. Even if I managed to succeed in affecting his substance, nothing in his outlook would change. His soul would continue to call out to him and want to grab his attention, but he would also continue not to turn in its direction no matter what happened in such an experiment.

It became very clear to me, as a result of this request, which I eventually turned down, that it couldn't be a matter of forcing a higher level down into a lower one in order to satisfy human reason. Rather, it's that we get started again on trying to get back up to those higher levels and into spheres where we simply just know and are and don't need any proof. Whoever wants conclusive proof feels no connection and no trust—in life, in their own soul, and in the higher order. Understanding will never capture this sense of the unbelievable and the limitless that we are. In this respect, it's like a mystical experience for which understanding will never find adequate descriptive words.

During my workshops on spiritual regression, it often happened that a participant came up with some facts of historical proof of their prior regression experiences. In my regression practice, the desire for verification surfaces only rarely. Proof is relatively unimportant to most of my clients. For them, it is much more about their personal experience and what they can take away from the regression in terms of benefits, assistance, and a new and rich perspective on their life today.

Evolution Through Joy

In the end, everything comes down to this wonderful common denominator. Initially much has to be learned through pain and suffering. This gets a person started, makes them ask questions, make decisions, undergo changes, try out new things, and develop desires. Then there comes a point on the path of evolution where you learn that you have free will and can get even further through joy.

At some point a soul has had enough of suffering in a human body, and perhaps it might even start to get a bit boring. It's like in a relationship in which there are some long-standing issues. As long as you are suffering and getting angry, or you want to stay angry with the other person and draw a certain satisfaction from that, you remain caught up in it all and nothing changes. Gradually, however, you start to know in advance what the other person is going to do and say; it hardly hurts anymore, but it's getting increasingly tedious. So you ask yourself, "Is there actually something more, something beautiful and meaningful in my life?" Then you can change the relationship for the better, or just move on.

Should I Be Happy?

Most of the blocks in our lives have one single cause: we don't permit ourselves to be happy and satisfied.

The fundamental mistake committed by so many people is to believe that our surroundings have to be a certain way and we have to have achieved certain external things in order to be happy. As a result of this, many people doubt themselves and think that they don't deserve to be happy. They distrust themselves and consider their need to live in a state of joy to be egoistic. They believe that having knowledge of the suffering of others forbids them from feeling good themselves. What a fateful error, and yet this determines the lives of so many people!

After all the regressions I have undergone and have accompanied others on, and in this intensive contact with the spirit world, I can formulate this one basic principle: it's all about bringing the soul consciousness of our divine essence to Earth. I don't mean some kind of superficial joy or malicious gloating, but a true, deep, and luminous inner joy that comes from the soul.

"But I did everything right! And I didn't do anything mean to anyone, either!" So said the man standing as a soul before his spirit guide, who was looking at him very sternly. "The important thing, though, is that you didn't live fully, even though you had everything, it all went well, and everything was under control."

The man didn't understand. "What was it then?" he asked.

"Joy. Why didn't you live with joy? Why didn't you enjoy your happiness?"

The soul understood. That was its aim and that's what it wanted to experience on Earth.

The soul is full of creativity and exuberance. It wants to experience this with others and explore its uniqueness. Anything that is blocked and messed up stops existing in the experience of real joy.

There are often strange fears that stand in the way of our own joie de vivre. Many people have to learn to grasp that living in a material world and collecting experiences there doesn't mean that spiritually they are not yet at a particularly high level. One shouldn't regard the material levels of life as something inferior, as things that have to be overcome.

It was our wish to incarnate and we are here of our own free will, because being human on this earth is something unbelievably beautiful and fascinating that enriches our souls a great deal. To experience being in a physical body, to learn how it works, and to create your life just as you want it to be, with all its creative possibilities and with a soul consciousness, is a gift and a great and wonderful adventure.

I have often seen clients who say before their regression, "I am probably now in my last incarnation, as I find it so awful here. Nothing's any fun, everything looks gray to me, and my whole life is tedious. I long to get away from the world." Such a statement is actually a sign that the soul still has to come back to Earth many more times. It is possible, however, that a person with a mature soul can also get tangled up in their early years and only find their way out of that entanglement when they are older.

Some might say, "I am so happy to be here. I thank God for every day that I can live on this earth. Everything I can do here, everything I can experience and discover, is so wonderful and exciting! I feel such love for all beings, for all that is. There's a quiet rejoicing in me." With people like this, the cycle of reincarnation is perhaps truly drawing to a close. Such a deep joy in life and love is a sign of great spiritual maturity.

In our culture it is widely believed that one can obtain a place in heaven through endurance and acquiescence. Then, however, you will return to the spirit world as a soul and have to say, "I did not take risks. I let my qualities lie fallow and eked out a joyless existence. And I still believed that this was making me a good person and I was going to be rewarded for it in the afterlife! I didn't pay attention to my life tasks and I haven't fulfilled them."

Some souls also learn in the spirit world to produce matter through pure thought power. One client experienced this during a session and, while doing it, began to glow with joy. I asked what he was doing and he answered, "I am making small bowls out of energy." He was filled with enthusiasm while doing it and told me that he was being forced by his parents in this current life to study economics, even though he was very keen to become a potter. He found his work in the marketing department of a large company deeply unsatisfying; it just wasn't right for him. After the session, the young man was firmly resolved to learn to be a potter and to become financially self-sufficient.

The soul always speaks through happiness and unhappiness. Unhappiness says, "Stop, wrong way!" Happiness says, "Good, keep going!" It is of tremendous importance that we recognize that through our thoughts and feelings we invite the corresponding events into our lives. In this way we create, as it were, an energy field all around us that works like a magnet. If we don't like something, we should turn as soon as possible toward what we actually want instead. We need to imagine it with great intensity, until we can feel the joy of it. Thus we consciously create the reality that we desire. If we continue to preoccupy ourselves instead with thoughts and feelings that are unpleasant to us, then these bad events will manifest themselves.

Joy always brings forth those critics who are of the opinion that if we only ever live and act from joy, the result will be total chaos because everyone will act out of selfishness and will exploit others. In fact, the opposite is the case, as compassion and a willingness to take responsibility arise from true joy. If I am happy and that joy is deep and genuine, I also want things to be good for others, and I will get on well with other beings and other things because otherwise I will lose that feeling of joy. Compassion and love for one's fellow human beings are the result of joy. Our truly good character traits come to the fore not through guilt and suffering, but through joy.

Living with Joy

Many people live like a leaf blowing in the wind: if something good happens, they feel good, and if something horrible happens, they feel horrible. This endless going back and forth is a terrible condition, as it seems like you are helplessly at the mercy of external conditions.

You learn gradually in the course of your life to end this cycle by changing yourself. You realize that joy in the outside world can remind you of the joy inside. The sadness and anger that are caused by an external event are closely connected to the sadness and anger in your inner landscape. Something on the inside is in resonance with the outside; otherwise you just wouldn't be able to feel it. Your feelings are your own, but they were also in existence already.

With increasing awareness, you start to recognize that you can decide for yourself how you are going to react to something. It is not necessary to feel bad because of an unpleasant event. When you begin to grasp this and practice it in your daily life, then external objects lose their sharpness at least initially. You detach yourself from your own dependence on the circumstances that exist in that moment. You simply take along with you the good and you leave what's unpleasant alone. You consciously turn toward what gives you pleasure. Interestingly, more and more good things then start to come into your life. That doesn't mean you have to leave everything just as it is now. You can also say no to things and then carry on in an appropriate manner.

The path of self-development teaches you to be more independent of your emotions. They can be used as signposts for constructive decision making, as long as you don't identify with them. There will still be situations for someone whose consciousness is growing where they have the feeling that this definitely isn't working and they are utterly at the mercy of their emotions. However, at the same time they notice that everything actually seems to be going much better. In the past, certain experiences would have thrown them completely off track, whereas now they just smile.

Take anger, for example. If you do manage to become more self-aware in such moment, you will see, from this higher perspective, that somewhere further down a part of you is raging, quarreling with itself and with the world. Then you can ask yourself what you can do with this part of your personality to soothe itself and relax. In this way you come more and more into harmony with the soul. You can quiet down and realize that anger would like to teach you something—perhaps to maintain better boundaries and express yourself more. If you did that, you would not need to get so angry.

This helpful technique of observing your own actions from outside and from a distance can help every mentally healthy person get up to a certain level. You can't do it as a small child, but you can develop it gradually as a youth and an adult.

There are also people who are happy and satisfied in more of an unconscious way. These are often very modest people who do straightforward jobs and whose circumstances are modest. Sometimes fate has dealt them some serious blows, but they move on from them well. You can sense that there is an experienced soul hidden there. They treat life at face value and don't focus constantly on themselves.

In a past life, one client of mine saw himself as a female African farmer who did everything moving rhythmically and elatedly, like a dancer. My client learned from this how fascinating it can be to express yourself through your body. He didn't have to have a specific reason or even a partner to do this. Just the movement, the sense of being in one's own body, was what this woman felt to be the greatest happiness of her earthly existence.

It can be such a wonderful experience to live on Earth! The more you are aware of this, the more you will feel the joy that already dwells in you. You will create your external conditions rather than surrender to them. You will discover how you can creatively weave your own life circumstances through your thoughts and feelings. The sense of being able to give something to other people, animals, and nature and of being able to pass on some of your own happiness will then fill you with the greatest satisfaction.

All Is One

A client came into the spirit world after her death in a past life. I asked her whether her spirit guide was there to greet her. She told me, "No, there is no spirit guide. We are all one. There is no separation between me and him. All these subdivisions and separations only exist in our concepts on Earth. In reality there is no separation, either between one human being and another or among animals or stars. It is all one." The client could clearly feel this deep wisdom when she experienced herself as a soul. However, I did ask her to take a look around the spirit world as best she could, as it does permit distinctions to be made, and to make contact with her spirit guide.

As long as we live on Earth, it makes sense to keep in place the reality that it is polarized. Of course it is even better when we know at the same time about the true state of being without separation and division. On Earth, however, we experience things as separate from us, and this is the framework in which we make our discoveries. This client also benefited from her spirit guide for her future life. She now sensed him as a formless, radiating white-golden light, with which she could exchange thoughts.

The deeper we experience the spiritual levels, the clearer it becomes for us how constrained our understanding actually is. It can only think in polarities and won't go beyond that because it finds it impossible. Trying to capture certain experiences or discoveries in words can overwhelm us—until we realize that they just don't need words. That which can be expressed, even when this "only" happens through words, can be a gift for someone else; it can strike a chord in a person who also carries this whole universe inside them. So just for this very reason, the polar possibilities, the "two-dimensional" options of thinking and speaking, are worthwhile and sensible on Earth. However, they can never replace personal experience, but can just direct you there, like a bridge. Clients often say to me during their trance that they just can't describe to me in words what they are going through in the spirit world, and that they would rather stay silent and just feel it. Yet even from the three sentences that I might extract from them, and from what comes streaming across from them on a more energetic level, I do get a sense of the special experience they have just had.

These wonderful feelings or states of being that one can experience in the spirit world are not so easy to have on Earth. Perhaps we might still experience them every once in a while in small doses. These can be moments in which we watch a beetle as if spellbound, observe the constellations in the heavens, or perhaps notice the wonder of a simple straw and how it can carry liquid out of a container and into a human body. Time stands still, and we experience a reverential wonder before the splendor and love of creation.

chapter fifteen

Twenty Case Examples from My Practice

I now present the following twenty cases from my regression practice so that you can immerse yourself even deeper emotionally into the theme of spiritual regression. The clients' names and birth dates, as well as the precise facts about their past lives, have been changed to protect the individuals' identities, but this doesn't distort the meaning of the actual content. These examples provide only a short snippet from each session. However, they vividly illustrate how this spiritual and therapeutic work operates and how a person can gain a totally new perspective on their life through a regression.

In the following case examples, "Cl." means client and "U.D." means Ursula Demarmels. The themes that are covered here should be relevant for most people at some point in their lives.

Paul L.—Less Is Often More

For some people, a regression awakens above all a long-forgotten sense of vitality and joie de vivre. That's how it appeared to me in the case of Paul L. Even while sitting down, he would huff and puff like a steam train, even though he had only just turned thirty-two. He was carrying at least ninety pounds of excess weight, and his doctor had advised him to change his lifestyle as a matter of urgency. Paul was a comfort eater. He looked oppressed and powerless. Asked about his history, he said that he was the youngest child and the black sheep in a successful family of doctors. He studied relatively hard in school, and when he turned eleven, he was sent to boarding school, where he was required to get good marks. From that point on, there was no time for sports, which up to that point he had loved doing.

He gave up on his medical studies after two terms. At the time of the regression, Paul was an accountant in a well-known firm—something that he enjoyed, even if his siblings, who were all respected doctors, would continually tease him about it. In his spare time, instead of relaxing, he would do the books for his father and his siblings, and he would have to listen to them tell him that he could be making the same amount of money as them if he wasn't so lazy.

The client had hardly even started looking at his past life when he called out enthusiastically:

Cl.: I'm so strong! I'm vigorous and powerful! And what muscles! Having a body like this is a great feeling!

U.D.: (*Laughing.*) So take this feeling deep within now. Breathe it into all your cells. How is that working?

Cl.: (*Breathing deeply.*) Yes. Wonderful!

U.D.: Who are you there? What are you doing?

Cl.: (*Eagerly.*) I am a stonemason. Eighteen years old perhaps. My name is Sandrino. My family sent me away at age thirteen to earn money. I enjoy working with stone.

U.D.: And where is this?

Cl.: In Italy. It's around the year 1050. We are building a nobleman's palace. It's going to be big. We'll never finish it! (*Cheerfully.*) I have got a job for life!

U.D.: How is your life? Do you feel contented?

Cl.: Yes, it's good. It can often be very demanding, but I enjoy it. What a lovely building! And I am so young and strong. It's wonderful. Perhaps this'll never get finished. But we'll keep building—in peace and undisturbed and using my strength and abilities.

The next scene to emerge in Sandrino's life also happened to be the last: around age twenty, he fell to his death from the scaffolding. A little later he noticed his spirit guide, who gathered him up and accompanied him up to the spirit world.

On the treatment couch, Paul seemed revitalized. He was bubbling with new ideas for how he could change things in his life as it existed today: he wanted to play the guitar more, to walk in the forest, and to visit a thermal spa. He would now allow himself more free time, and he seemed determined to enjoy it.

Cl.: I'm satisfied with my life as an accountant. That's enough for me. I'm not going to let anyone convince me that I'm a failure anymore.

U.D.: Who tries to tell you that?

Cl.: My family. (*Pause.*) You can't measure how happy you are just by money! I think I have to shut my ears to all that. I would prefer to break off contact. I'm not going to look after their accounts anymore. That's just turned into an extra part-time job! I won't do it now. I need this time for myself, for my own private life.

Ilka J.—Not Without You

This thirty-six-year-old dentist seemed to be a person with both feet planted firmly on the ground. However, Ilka felt lonely and incapable of forming deeper relationships. Since she had already tried a few different therapeutic approaches, she knew that nothing traumatic had happened in her childhood or adolescence. Now, though, she hoped to find a reason from her past life for this nagging and unwanted aloneness.

In our session, there was no doubt that we almost immediately stumbled across the same theme: loneliness. In a previous life Ilka found herself crouching in a dark room as a forty-one-year-old woman named Margret, feeling abandoned and without any joy in life. She took the year to be 1798. It turned out that she had worked as a tutor and chaperone for some wealthy families in England. Margret was quite happy with this. When she was thirty, she got to know a boat builder. They had met on a walk along the wild and romantic chalk cliffs of Wales, not far from where Margret lived. Their relationship was passionate and happy, even though she had to keep it a secret from her employers. Some years later, however, the boat builder was found drowned on the beach. In her pain, Margret withdrew from everything, neglected her work, was consequently dismissed, and from that point ended up sitting in her room staring blankly into space.

Cl.: I am going to the cliffs.

U.D.: Yes. (*Pause.*) What next?

Cl.: I am going right to the edge. The sea is crashing below me. (*Pause.*) I am jumping off.

U.D.: Hmm. (*Very long pause.*) And next?

Cl.: My body is lying there, on the rocks. I see it lying right at the bottom, completely smashed to pieces. I am going straight past it, and I am rising up. (*Happy and surprised.*) Oh, there's my friend! He's waiting for me!

A little later the spirit guide receives Margret, but then leads her straight away one more time back down to her body on the ground, so that she can learn the lesson of her earthly existence.

U.D.: And what was it about your death? The leap from the cliffs?

Cl.: (*Trembling.*) I should have been able to learn how to live better with myself and also to love other people.

U.D.: So suicide wasn't such a good idea?

Cl.: It was okay, but I should have been able to learn.

U.D.: Take a look at your spirit guide. What did he make of you committing suicide because your friend wasn't there anymore? (*Pause.*) Look closely. Does he think it's good?

Cl.: No, he has a different opinion. It wasn't good. He wanted me to see it through … Life, that is …

U.D.: Every life is a great opportunity, isn't it?

Cl.: Yes. I … I threw it all away.

U.D.: Hmm. (*Long pause.*) Take a good deep breath. (*Pause.*) Ask your spirit guide: Was it part of your life plan as Margret for your beloved to die and for you then to stay on the earth? Should you have learned to continue to get involved with other people even after this cruel blow of fate?

Cl.: Yes, and I was thinking it was really easy!

Ilka realized that in her life today, she was just continuing to do what she had done in her earlier one. She let no one get close to her out of a fear that a beloved person might die or abandon her. But now that the cause of this was clearer to her, and she also recognized that Margret's life plan was not to retreat, she felt almost liberated. She also knew that leave-taking was still a part of life, and anyway, it's not forever. Retreat and running away are not good solutions.

Xaver T.—Success Has Two Faces

Cl.: (*Astounded.*) This girl, this uneducated and developmentally disabled Marie, was much happier than I am today! She had contentment and love in her heart!

This important declaration by my client was the decisive turning point in his regression process. When the forty-four-year-old Xaver T. entered my office, he acted so erratically and aggressively that I actually considered turning him away.

Almost immediately he started baiting me, and to do so he used all sorts of clever mind games, but I didn't rise to the bait. Little by little, however, the reason he had come to me started to become clear. As a brilliant lawyer, he had gained the admiration of his colleagues, the fear of his opponents, a lot of money, plus the feeling of great power. "I am a winner," he announced proudly, "and whether or not they were guilty, all my clients were cleared in court and it was my opponent who had to pay up."

Then, however, he started being tormented by horrible dreams in which dozens of hands were trying to pull him underwater. At age forty-three, he suffered a heart attack. After that, he tried picking himself back up and returning to the courtroom, but his efforts were in vain.

Xaver related how, one night after yet another nightmare, he was at a total loss as to what he should do next. "That was when I started to pray for help. And now I am sitting here with you, which was what a friend recommended to me the very next day." Thus he concluded his story, with a sarcastic undertone that was hard to miss.

We began with the regression. The first scene Xaver picked up from his past life was hideous. It took us a long time to figure out what was happening, as he found it hard to express himself as the woman he was at the time. Eventually it became clear that she was being given electric shocks in the hope that they would make her "normal" again. Xaver was experiencing life as a developmentally disabled young woman in the late 1940s.

Until she was around eighteen, Marie lived in an Austrian town and she wandered cheerfully around the streets while people made all sorts of nasty jokes at her expense—although in general she really didn't take them that way. She laughed along in a carefree fashion. However, her parents died and they had loved her very much and looked after her. She had to move in with her brother's family in the suburbs. There they were ashamed of her "otherness." Her sister-in-law forbade the children from playing with her, and she was even beaten on many occasions. (I had to change her words from sometimes garbled fragments into much clearer and comprehensible language.)

Cl.: I am afraid.

U.D.: Of what?

Cl.: I am hiding behind a tree.

U.D.: Why? Does someone want to do something mean to you?

Cl.: Everyone is chasing me away. And hitting me.

U.D.: How do you feel?

Cl.: Sad. Why am I not allowed to play with the children? (*Pause.*) There's a bird singing in the tree. (*Laughs happily.*) It's so cheerful.

I invited Xaver to move on to the end of Marie's life. He saw himself as a bedraggled woman living in a mental asylum. This was also where she was given the electric shocks.

U.D.: How are you?

Cl.: Quite good. They are leaving me alone now. (*Pause.*)
   I am still alone.

U.D.: How is that for you?

Cl.: I'd like to laugh. Laugh again. But I am very tired. Dead
   tired.

Marie died in this institution under wretched conditions.
When Xaver talked to his spirit guide about it and asked why
he had just been shown this life, he was overwhelmed by his
feelings. To my surprise, he said:

Cl.: It's all about the small joys. Marie had barely even struggled against things. Not once was she angry. She knew
   almost nothing, but she was always cheerful, even though
   other people were so nasty to her.

U.D.: What can you take from this life today, in your life as
   Xaver?

Cl.: (*In an outburst.*) I feel like I am at the end! My body, my
   nerves, all the dreams I had for the future! What can I
   expect next? (*Pause.*) This more sensitive side, this gentle,
   naive, loving side … I just never noticed it before.

U.D.: Perhaps there is something to this. Why don't you ask
   your spirit guide?

Cl.: He is showing me that figure of Justice with her scales
   and her blindfold, like a living statue. The scales—they
   connect the two sides, the struggling and the gentle ones.
   It's a question of justice. Yes, I have just gotten the feeling

that I came to Earth for that reason: to help the weaker ones and fight injustice.

U.D.: You've got the perfect job for that, haven't you?

Cl.: Oh, yes. Yes, I have. Until now, I have taken whatever work came along. Winning the hopeless cases ... acquitting the guilty ones. (*Pause.*) I can now do things differently ... look elsewhere for my clients. More than anything else, it'll be about justice, and where it is failing and where I can bring it about. It's as if I can then stand up for another Marie, so she can live a decent and happy life.

U.D.: That sounds good. You can use your exceptional skills to fulfill your life's purpose. In so doing, you will also be doing something good for society.

Cl.: (*Surprised.*) That's quite a different way of looking at things: putting justice and truth first. Not so much on winning at any price. It's more about higher values. Then I think I can start enjoying things more. But I will need a lot of strength.

U.D.: And what might help you with that?

Cl.: (*After a pause.*) Perhaps ... praying again. Asking for help. To the heavens, as it were.

U.D.: That sounds very good. Praying is better than just asking, because it's also a way of giving thanks and of connecting with the divine. And listening—for what the answer to your prayer actually sounds like.

Cl.: Yes, I can try that.

Once again I led Xaver through a scene in which the girl Marie was unequivocally happy. Then I guided him to anchor this feeling in his current life as Xaver, using deep breathing. Finally his spirit guide enveloped him for a few minutes with his energy, to send him confidence and a deep feeling of acceptance. I led a greatly changed man out of my regression practice that day. He looked more relaxed and positive, and I wished from my heart that he could integrate what had seemed so important in our session into the rest of his life.

Maria K.—Life under the Pressure to Achieve

Tomboyish, courteous, and a bit frazzled—that is how I saw Maria K. at the start of our session. The thirty-three-year-old owner of a motor vehicle repair shop had already achieved a great deal in her young life, and she had a lot more in front of her.

She needed to make improvements to the repair shop, although her husband, who taught German and music, thought it wasn't necessary. He tried without success to curb his wife's constant drive to achieve. Maria wanted to raise their daughter to be a thoroughly modern young woman, to be equally skilled both technically and musically, and the eight-year-old's daily routine was overloaded with lessons. The child was often irritable and had trouble sleeping. Maria came to me because she wanted to access a deeper potential through regression and was looking for ways to find more energy for her daughter and for all her various projects.

She experienced herself during World War II as a soldier named Fritz who left his family behind, was wounded in the trenches, spent several years in captivity, and then finally returned home. Once there, he discovered that his farm, which was beside the Lüneburg Heath, had survived the war undamaged, and if anything had become even more beautiful, as his now grown-up son and wife had looked after it so well. In the years that followed, the farm continued to flourish, they acquired even more animals, and eventually they added a riding school. Fritz continued to work hard even though he had lost a leg and three fingers in the war. The family prospered. Then Fritz's life came to an end.

Cl.: I am lying in my sick bed.

U.D.: And then what happens?

Cl.: It's as if I am simply walking away, like through a veil. It's quite easy.

U.D.: Please stay in your body a bit longer! Is anyone with you? Your family?

Cl.: (*Haltingly.*) No ... They have things to do. They'll come along later. (*Pause.*) I don't want to die yet. It's horrible to ...

U.D.: What's horrible?

Cl.: I am waiting, but ... (*Cries.*) ... it won't be much longer.

U.D.: What's making you sad? Are you sad because the rest of your family isn't there? Or because you have to leave them?

Cl.: (*Sobbing.*) I wanted ... I wanted at least to hug them one last time. (*Pause.*)

U.D.: Where are you going after you die as Fritz?

Cl.: It's like an endless expanse. Everything is very light and easy. (*Pause.*) There are some people who are waiting for me. (*Cheerful.*) I know them!

U.D.: Who is there?

Cl.: Many souls. They are full of love. We have known each other for a long time.

U.D.: What do they look like?

Cl.: Like light, bright light, with no actual form, as such. It's … yes, it's my home.

U.D.: Enjoy it in peace.

Cl.: (*Pause, then laughter.*) It's crazy, all the laughter and the fun they are having. It's … so beautiful.

U.D.: Take this lightheartedness and joy deep within you.

After this liberating welcome to the spirit world, Maria took a look at her life as Fritz, together with her spirit guide. Maria quickly noticed that it was a good life on a purely material level. However, the whole area of interpersonal relationships had been neglected, as had the area of spirituality—that simply wasn't a theme that ran through this particular life. Above all, it caused her soul pain when it noticed that the animals, which were the main source of the family's livelihood, had been treated like inanimate objects. Fritz noticed right after his death that he had never had any feelings for them and that he had never perceived them as living beings. Furthermore, the client called out at one point, "We've sprayed so much poison on the fields! That's something that Fritz never thought twice about."

The message for Maria quickly became clear: more love, empathy, relaxation, and enjoyment—that was the gist of it. At first that seemed to be a tough challenge for the client, as it really didn't fit with the convictions by which she had lived her life up to that point. But then she realized that she could use her daughter's condition as a gauge to judge if she was on the right track. The girl was always cheerful and content unless her mother was pressuring her with ever greater expectations. Maria was starting to get the feeling that she should let the girl have more of a childhood and she should be playing with her rather than urging her forward all the time. She was now ready to let her daughter fulfill her most ardent wish and have a small pet. More than anything, Maria wanted the cheerful little girl inside her to come alive at last.

Martin C.—Yet This Love Still Remains

Despite several personal setbacks, Martin C. radiated a lot of joie de vivre. In private, the twenty-nine-year-old computer expert from a small town in Switzerland would contemplate various questions about ethics and spirituality. He was having more and more doubts about whether any of it made any sense, when his experiences were showing him that to all outward appearances he was wrong. He lost his mother at an early age, and in his teenage years he had a serious accident. He hadn't been able to find fulfillment through his work, and when he was twenty-six his beloved wife left him and was still trying to make his life difficult. The young man was not looking to blame outside events but tended instead to blame himself. However, he also seemed to be less and less convinced of this attitude as well. I had the impression that he was making it too hard for himself and that he hadn't yet uncovered the true meaning of it all.

In his previous life, Martin found himself back in a dark dungeon. He was a count named Michael, who was due to be burned at the stake the next day.

U.D.: Why are you imprisoned here? How did it happen?

Cl.: I challenged the bishop, the power of the bishop.

U.D.: Why?

Cl.: To set an example.

U.D.: What country are you in?

Cl.: Germany, around the twelfth century.

U.D.: And why did you want to set an example?

Cl.: Because the social contract between men and their patrons doesn't hold anymore. Everything is out of balance in the way men treat their fellow men.

U.D.: So what bad things are they doing then?

Cl.: The oppression of the serfs and the overall treatment of the peasants.

U.D.: Were you able to achieve anything?

Cl.: More than could be seen from the outside.

U.D.: More?

Cl.: Yes, more. I am sure of it. It was important. (*Pause.*) But sometimes I have doubts, too. They sent me a priest who was supposed to expound on the word of God to me. What a self-serving fool! (*Laughs bitterly.*) But then ... I started thinking, I have gotten myself into such a lousy situation ...

U.D.: What did you have doubts about?

Cl.: Well, maybe it was wrong ... I mean, to rebel like that.

U.D.: Did the priest say that to you?

Cl.: Yes, of course. (*Quietly.*) Perhaps he planted the doubt in my mind. He said I would be acting against God's orders.

U.D.: Let's see now how this life ended. Go to your last day as the count, the last minutes.

Cl.: They dressed me in a white robe, tied my hands behind my back, and led me to a pile of wood, the funeral pyre, which had been stacked up there with the stake in the middle ... I was tied up to it.

U.D.: Are you alone or are there others there?

Cl.: I'm alone. I'm the last one.

U.D.: There were others then?

Cl.: There were quite a few of us who stood up to the bishop. But they weren't taken prisoner like me—they were killed on the spot.

U.D.: And what's happening now?

Cl.: They are lighting the pyre.

U.D.: How is it for you?

Cl.: (*Surprised.*) I am feeling a lot of love. In spite of everything, I am feeling a lot of love ... (*Crying.*) This love still remains ...

U.D.: Are there people there? Spectators?

Cl.: Yes, there are a few spectators and the bishop is there too. He is sitting opposite me on his throne some distance away, with his followers. (*Slowly.*) But I've got so much love, for them too.

U.D.: Is there just love?

Cl.: It hurts a lot too.

U.D.: Yes.

Cl.: And there's also ... there's also such a feeling of hate.

U.D.: Yes.

Cl.: And above all a lot of sadness.

U.D.: Become aware of all these many and varied sensations and then observe how your life as Michael ends.

Cl.: I am trying to ... to breathe in these initial whitish, brownish-gray fumes very deeply as they rise up from the wet logs so that I will lose consciousness as quickly as possible.

U.D.: Is it working?

Cl.: Yes.

U.D.: Good. What's next?

Cl.: I am letting my body go.

U.D.: Okay ... How are you doing that?

Cl.: It's easy, just like taking a step to one side.

U.D.: How is it unfolding?

Cl.: I am watching what's happening. My guardian angel, my spirit guide, has come and she is positioned behind me, just to the left, and has put a hand on my shoulder.

U.D.: How does that feel?

Cl.: We are both watching the scene in front of us. There is a lot of sadness. (*Sobs.*) Because we have missed such a great

opportunity for people to restore some balance. (*Pause.*)
I am getting a great deal of energy from my spirit guide,
a lot … Everything that went wrong through this psychic
torture and all the stuff of the last few weeks—she made
it flow through my consciousness again, and because of
that, it's all going a lot better for me now.

U.D.: Great. Now take that deep into yourself.

Cl.: Even though it looks as if an opportunity might have
been wasted by these people, this whole thing has been
a lot more effective on a deeper level.

U.D.: Tell me more about this.

Cl.: (*Hesitantly.*) There's … there's more there than just me
and my light guide. There are many beings of light there.
This is how it is: All during this whole scenario, there had
been like a mourning bell tolling for all these beings. It's
been like an interior show of sadness. And even though
these people have been sitting so self-righteously on their
chairs, there's a lot of sorrow erupting in their hearts. And
at least this will help them all with their further development too.

In looking back at this life as Michael, Martin realized that
he had made himself pretty comfortable in his present-day
life but had also become very conformist and anxious. It had
become important for him to take more risks and be more
supportive of himself. It was time for him to pay attention to
his wise inner essence and to make more of his insights and
his greater visions in the everyday world—and furthermore,
as he himself said, "with complete commitment and without
this horrible self-doubt. Outward difficulties should not be

taken as some kind of proof that I am on the wrong path." I called upon him to get a sense of himself again as a light-filled and mature soul and to connect with it through his current conscious existence as Martin, so that he can then be led by it.

In that previous life, Martin's personal well-being was not an issue. He understood quite clearly that he'd had an opportunity to make a contribution to the general good of all, to act as a positive reformer in the sweep of history. Martin also recognized this as his life's work today.

Andrea K.—The Humility of the Heart

Already during her time in the womb—at least as she experienced it during the first phase of her regression—Andrea K. had the feeling that she didn't really want to be on the earth. She struggled against it as desperately and felt powerless. I only managed to make brief contact with the soul; it knew, though, that it was coming voluntarily.

This client, a forty-six-year-old woman, was swept into my practice as a self-righteous and bossy therapist from Munich who already considered herself more or less enlightened. Her dismissive attitude toward other people, nature, animals, and plants was remarkably strong. When questioned about this, she explained to me that she was ultimately concerned only with the more exalted levels of existence. Once she had let loose an infinite procession of phrases from the esoteric scene, she then said despondently that none of her relationships had fulfilled her at all, that she felt empty and disappointed, and that for some time she had even been considering suicide. She felt like she hadn't been made for this earth.

In her past life, she saw herself as a hermit in the Indian Himalayas, dressed in just a robe and without possessions, living in a cave—alone.

Cl.: I am satisfied with myself. I am happy being on my own, but…

U.D.: But what?

Cl.: … there's just no one there.

U.D.: Do you miss having someone else there?

Cl.: (*Very quietly.*) Yes.

We went further back into that life. As the man in the Himalayan cave, he (Andrea) initially felt exceptionally strong, with radiant, vibrating chakras in the lower half of his body, and with a deep sense of connection with all of existence. Then he lived for a few years with a woman who eventually left him to return to live a normal, secular life. He did not want to go with her, and after that, he lost all his power and optimism.

Cl.: I am dying of a broken heart. That's how it feels.

U.D.: What has broken your heart?

Cl.: The woman who left me. I never intended to enter into a relationship. People are unpredictable and selfish.

U.D.: Hmm.

Cl.: I have also stopped glowing. I have lost my power.

After death, the hermit's soul climbed up into the spirit world and, together with its spirit guide, reviewed all the stages of that life one more time.

Cl.: Because of that woman, I gave away my spirituality. I didn't cultivate it anymore, and because of that, it was lost.

U.D.: What did you learn in this life or because of this life?

Cl.: Well, that sometimes it doesn't take much to slide down from a lofty, pure, and bright place into hell.

U.D.: Hmm.

Cl.: (*With a sudden exclamation.*) In which case, my condition was probably not so perfect after all! (*Pause.*) I was only … only fooling myself.

U.D.: Yes, that's a good realization.

Cl.: All I want is to get it back and hang on to it.

U.D.: Hang on to what, exactly?

Cl.: That vibrant force in my chakras.

U.D.: Now let's take another look at what happened back then. You have conceded that someone external can take this power from you, or was it not like that?

Cl.: (*Hesitantly.*) I gave away my power myself. There was something missing … in me.

U.D.: Yes. And then what?

Cl.: (*Faltering.*) There was no … my heart was missing. The fourth chakra, I wasn't there yet. It wasn't the woman's fault. (*Pause.*) That's what I would really like to develop.

The heart has to be there, in order to live. (*Cries for a long time.*)

By the end of the session, I had taken Andrea back again to the state she experienced as a hermit of feeling very much at ease and powerful. I gave her guidance on how to integrate these energies into her everyday life so that she could build on them and master her life's project: to find her heart's love. I had the feeling that after the session I was leaving behind a much softer woman. She smiled, somewhat unsure of herself and with a face wet with tears. With a few words she was able to capture how she now felt: "moved and humbled."

Peter M.—In a Rush of Force and Authority

Cl.: We are running through a dark woods, another man and I. I'm his boss, I think. He seems to cower whenever I look at him.

U.D.: Aha. Who are you? Why do you think you are running through the woods?

Cl.: It's nighttime. There's a house with only a woman in it.

U.D.: And?

Cl.: We are robbers. Yes, I am a robber.

U.D.: Are you going to break into the house?

Cl.: Yes. There's food there and there must also be a bit of money ... oh no, the woman is on her own. A young woman.

U.D.: Do you have a weapon?

Cl.: A thick wooden club.

U.D.: How do you feel?

Cl.: Strong. I feel very good. I am so fired up ... this break-in ... our prey ... the woman who belongs to me ...

U.D.: Do you think that this woman is the prey?

Cl.: Yes, that's always the case!

U.D.: How do you feel about that?

Cl.: I am strong ... I just don't think about it at all.

U.D.: What's happening now?

Cl.: We are at the house. There's just one light on. Everything's quiet.

U.D.: And then?

Cl.: Suddenly I am going very fast. I can feel my strength, how it's all coiled up inside me. What a strong feeling! Nothing can stop me now. I start to scream, then I run up to the door and crash into it. (*Bewildered.*) But the door had already opened on its own. What's going on? I fall on to the floor inside the house. Then there's a blow to the head.

U.D.: What sort of blow?

Cl.: I don't know, but it hurts like hell. (*Pause.*) It's all over. I see myself just lying there. The body ... I am floating above it. My mate's run away. (*Shocked and stunned.*) A large man is dragging my body outside.

Peter M., a smart and overly self-confident real estate agent from Hamburg, had found himself back in his life as a robber in the eighteenth century in what is now the Czech Republic. Just when it looked like it was going to go so well for him, he was killed. The sense of shock and disappointment he felt was immediately apparent. It wasn't his first regression, and again and again he would be confronted with the issue of violence. Initially he couldn't understand its connection with his current life, as this rather slender man was not a bully, nor did he ever recall being assaulted himself. In reviewing the events he had just reexperienced, it all became somewhat clearer.

Cl.: I considered myself to be invincible, and I took everything that I wanted for myself.

U.D.: Hmm.

Cl.: And now, when I look at it from the point of view of a soul, it hurts.

U.D.: Hmm.

Cl.: I am bitterly disappointed in myself. (*Cries.*)

U.D.: Yes, indeed. (*Pause.*) What have you learned now that you have looked back at it?

Cl.: It's painful and pointless, to put it bluntly. This violence … it has no point. (*Pause.*) It destroys, it breaks everything, it makes you lonely. It's so pointless and it's not how life is supposed to be. I can feel that now.

U.D.: Yes, now you feel it as a soul.

Cl.: (*Quietly.*) This frenzy of violence, it was pleasurable for me, over and over again and across many lifetimes. But it didn't bring me anything. Not really, just a rush, and then after that …

U.D.: How is that for you today? Get into contact with your spirit guide.

Cl.: No violence. It's much better. I've learned. (*Pause.*) My spirit guide looks so serious. Oh! But ... I ... yes, I am doing it seemingly different today, but it is also similar in a way.

U.D.: What do you mean? What are you doing today that's similar?

Cl.: I still want to be invincible and strong ... and have admiration. No one must know that I feel wounded ... Like for example when my wife is away ... with someone else. I do it with my intelligence, with my knowledge and even ... with esoteric matters. I let myself be admired for it. I am mysterious. It's a power play, as it was then. Only now without a club.

In this sitting, sixty-four-year-old Peter was made aware of how much he had cut himself off from his own true feelings and also from his fellow human beings. His wife had left him seven years earlier, and he had buried his bitter disappointment about it deep inside. Consequently, he would outwardly play the macho man who had everything under control. However, he had never managed to form another relationship since and would describe sex as a dirty pursuit. I was very happy to receive a letter from him around a year after this sitting in which he described how then he had since gotten together with a very dear woman. I could read between the lines that he had become a happy man who enjoyed the simple pleasures in life—a different man from the one I had gotten to know earlier.

Markus W.—Everything in the Proper Flow

At age twenty-seven, Markus W. was in his last year of training as a restaurateur, worked as a Meals on Wheels driver,
sang in a band, and with his life partner was preparing for the
opening of their own restaurant. It would be a kind of artsy
cafe in an Austrian provincial town, serving their own unique
culinary creations using organic ingredients. He was full of
energy and joie de vivre as he told me about this project.

Markus is a good example of the sort of client who above
all takes the regression as a validation that he is on the right
path. As he stated, "I am so fascinated by the possibilities offered by regression that I really want to experience one for
myself. It's important for me to learn more about myself and
about life." A regression presents such clients with a deeply felt
knowledge that we can all find our place in the greater order,
one in which we can wholeheartedly place our trust. During
the regression, we initially lingered for a while in the time
when Markus was still in the womb:

Cl.: There is this throbbing. The heart is …

U.D.: Yes.

Cl.: … thump, thump …

U.D.: Take a look at where your mother is. Is she outdoors
or is she in the house?

Cl.: Outdoors.

U.D.: What is she doing?

Cl.: She's standing by the garden fence talking with another
woman. The sun is out. And she has brown hair, quite
long, with a blue dress and a big belly.

U.D.: What do you look like? Can you describe yourself?

Cl.: I can't see myself. But I see her, from above and at an angle. I can float—excellent! I am not there inside her anymore. (*Pause.*) There's my spirit guide.

U.D.: How do you know it's him?

Cl.: It's like there's a light beside me and it's always there. I am also made out of light right now.

U.D.: What do you know about the life that lies before you? What sort of life will it be?

Cl.: It's going to be stressful, a lot going on.

U.D.: Do you know why?

Cl.: Many challenges. And fears.

U.D.: What have you resolved to do? What do you know of your life goals and life lessons?

Cl.: (*Deep in contemplation.*) Yes, I want to feel love. Love between people. Which comes from the heart, without conventions—those conventions that always block things out.

U.D.: That's nice.

Cl.: I really want to touch people's hearts.

When I asked Markus later whether he thought he'd be able to find that from now on in his life, he said yes. "The challenges…that was primarily about being gay. Accepting that wasn't easy, but I didn't want to live a lie."

After the time in the womb, I guided Markus into a past life. He found himself to be a Buddhist nun in the north of

Japan at some point in the sixteenth century. She was in her mid-seventies and looking back on her life.

Cl.: I am at peace. That's what I have been looking for. When I am sitting here on this mountain, playing my flute and looking down across the land, I feel very good.

U.D.: Are you comfortable in yourself?

Cl.: (*Hesitantly.*) I have missed out a bit on seeing the world. I think I haven't seen much of it, and there's a lot I haven't experienced.

U.D.: Do you regret it?

Cl.: Not really. Sometimes now it's just like a longing. (*Pause.*) But that's okay.

U.D.: Take a deep breath and go on to the next thing in this life that wants to emerge.

Cl.: I see myself as an old lady, about eighty-four years old.

U.D.: How is it going for you now? Are you still sprightly? Or are you ill and tired?

Cl.: Sprightly. But I am a bit hunched over now.

U.D.: Are you still in the monastery?

Cl.: Yes. I am at the spring, collecting water. Then back to the kitchen, to start the fire and do the cooking. (*Pause.*) I am saying my prayers all the time.

U.D.: How are you feeling now, deep inside?

Cl.: I have found perfect peace in my life. It was a very good life, with much peace in my heart. I now understand the way things unfold much better.

After the nun's death, Markus experienced the spirit world again as a soul. His spirit guide led him into a vast hall.

Cl.: This room has an enormous window, like a glass cupola. It's like … the universe, the stars, the planets … but it feels to me like it's all in this one room.

U.D.: What does that mean to you?

Cl.: The spirit guide is showing me that every being in the universe has its place. Everyone follows their given task, which is to serve the greater good, and thus to keep developing further.

U.D.: Do you know your place in life, as Markus, that is?

Cl.: (*After a pause.*) My place is always exactly where I am already and where I can give my best, which is exactly what is coming from my heart.

Marianne U.—In Spite of Everything

Marianne U. was forty-six when she came to me, a wiry and careworn-looking woman with a loud voice, living in a village near Konstanz in Germany. She wanted to give up her job as a shop assistant, which she didn't like, in order to be able to help other people in some kind of therapeutic way. She was using the regression to find a place to start. In her previous life, she found herself to be a Jewish lawyer in a provincial town in Brandenburg during World War II. He, his family, and his neighbors had just been captured by the Nazis.

Cl.: An SS man is coming up to us. He is staring at me in a strange way.

U.D.: What do you mean by that?

Cl.: He ... It's disgust!

U.D.: What, that he's expressing, or do you feel disgust?

Cl.: Him. It's as if he is looking at dirt. So ice cold.

U.D.: What's happening?

Cl.: (*Hesitantly.*) They are driving us into a barn. Six soldiers with weapons.

U.D.: And more ...

Cl.: They are going to shoot us now. They are lining us up in a row. Jakob, my son, next to me ... and the neighbors, and two girls ... they are crying.

U.D.: How do you feel?

Cl.: I feel afraid, but I also hope that it's over soon ...

U.D.: Yes.

Cl.: Now Jakob is standing very close to me.

U.D.: Can you take hold of him?

Cl.: Hmm. I have his hand. (*Suddenly bursts out.*) I hate these people! They are beasts!

U.D.: Go on.

Cl.: I hope it's over quickly. They are giving orders behind me. So cold and ... and harsh.

U.D.: What's happening?

Cl.: Guns firing ... the shots. I can hear it ... but somehow it doesn't really concern me.

U.D.: Hmm. Where are you?

Cl.: I am seeing it ... from above.

U.D.: Are you all dead now? Can you see your body?

Cl.: Yes. He is still alive. Just a little bit.

U.D.: Ah! So you got out early. Very good. That is very good.

Cl.: (*After a pause.*) They're clearing the bodies away now. Mine's completely lifeless as well now. I am dead.

U.D.: Can you see Jakob?

Cl.: He is now further up above me. He looks somewhat transparent.

U.D.: And how do you perceive yourself now?

Cl.: Transparent, too, an elongated form ... A kind of vortex is drawing me upward.

U.D.: Have you still got a human form or has that gone?

Cl.: It's like a narrow band. Bright.

U.D.: And how are you now?

Cl.: Light, free in some way.

Marianne understood that she had to learn to let go of those closest to her. Also, in times of danger, she wouldn't always be able to protect them, just as she hadn't been able to protect her son Jakob. But there is a much higher form of protection: the life after death.

U.D.: Is there something that you didn't do so well? How does it look now that you can look back on this previous life as a soul?

Cl.: I didn't believe all the talk.

U.D.: About the persecution of the Jews?

Cl.: Maybe we should have left.

U.D.: Take a look at the spirit guide. Did you ignore the danger?

Cl.: No, I didn't overlook anything. That's how it was. I don't need to reproach myself.

U.D.: Was there anything that didn't go quite so well?

Cl.: The anger right at the end.

U.D.: Before the shooting?

Cl.: That officer, his look… I hated him.

U.D.: Yes.

Cl.: I hung on to that hate and took it with me into this current life.

U.D.: Whatever a person hates, they can't really let go of. You then drag it around with you, even if the outward circumstances are completely different. Very important. So what can you learn from this for your life today?

Cl.: It's a question of this anger. Nowadays I prefer to be alone because … well, just in case I find myself relying on someone and he lets me down, then … the hate comes back. I don't want that!

U.D.: Let's take another look back: back then, as a young man who is going to be shot with his son. That is an exceptionally difficult situation … Perhaps you need to bring a bit more understanding to it.

Cl.: That's true. (*Pause.*) But … I suppose I might have been able to say to the officer, "You will do what is meant for you to do. It's yours." And instead of anger, there could have been the love there for my son … I could simply feel that …

U.D.: That would have been better, without question, but very difficult. (*Pause.*) Souls know no hatred; that only exists on the earth. If you bring your soul consciousness down to Earth, your hatred will evaporate. In the past, that didn't quite go right. Also, everything happened so quickly at the very end. You were dead soon afterward and you were in no position anymore to change your feelings. But today that whole issue seems to have returned. Today there is hate as well in…

Cl.: (*Interrupts, suddenly excited.*) Jakob! Jakob is my mother now!

U.D.: Look over to your spirit guide. Is that true?

Cl.: He is nodding his head. Yes, it's true.

U.D.: Is there a specific task that you both have to work through between you?

Cl.: I wouldn't know. (*Pause.*)

U.D.: Let your spirit guide help you with this.

Cl.: (*Astonished.*) He is showing me a picture of my father.

Marianne was suddenly aware of quite a different aspect of her current life: that the pivot and fulcrum of her everyday life was still in fact her father—a particularly uncaring and selfish man who had died eight years previously. The client lived in her mother's household, and both women would rail from dawn till dusk against their husband and father, whom they blamed for absolutely everything that went wrong in their lives. Marianne said that her feelings of hate for him grew stronger every day. According to her accounts, he was undeniably a man who had done a lot of bad things. However, she now noticed that she would regularly cling to her status as a wronged victim and that her father served as a convenient alibi for this. On the other hand, her mother would make veiled accusations to her: that she had only kept this uneasy marriage going so that her father wouldn't be taken from her. Thus Marianne was suspended in a state of guilty dependency with her mother. I suggested to the client, as a matter of urgency, that she focus on the positive things, instead of cursing her father.

When Marianne appeared eight weeks later for her second appointment, she seemed more cheerful and less reproachful toward her father and what had gone on between them. Even her current job didn't seem as bad as it had before. She could even laugh about it all, now that she was aware that she could no longer blame her dead father for everything. In a certain way, she still did so, but only from time to time, for the sake of her mother, who by her own account had supposedly suffered so much under him. However, after a further encounter with her spirit guide, Marianne soon saw that this was nonsense. After that second session she even timidly broached the idea that she could get her own flat, so that she could find out who she really was, independent of her father and mother.

Natalie D.—Hoping for Prince Charming

This thirty-four-year-old Parisian woman had been living for several years in Zürich. She had worked previously at the reception desk of a hotel, but since she had married, she hadn't had to work anymore. The client, who was very pretty but somewhat affected, was well prepared in advance for her regression appointment, at least in her own particular way: Natalie D. had with her a long list of everything about her husband that irritated her. His predecessor, the great love of her life, had abandoned her at a difficult time. Then she married this loving man, who could never do enough for her and only earned her ingratitude. She considered him responsible for her feeling unfulfilled and unhappy and grieved for the loss of the other man.

A fairly similar situation presented itself to Natalie in her previous life. She was a dancer in Damascus and loved a rich and handsome man. She was happy—she could experience her body as it danced, full of a lust for life and a thrilling eroticism. Then she became pregnant and the man left her. And again, even back then in the past, another man took her under his wing:

U.D.: Why did he accept you? Did he know that you were going to have a child?

Cl.: I had already had the child. He took me on, with the child. He knew that, yes.

U.D.: Was something like that customary in those days in Damascus?

Cl.: No, absolutely not! This is madness. It's a great demonstration of love on his part. (*Smiles proudly.*) I mean a lot to him.

Frightened, Natalie then stated that she was chasing after a romantic dream even then, and that she trampled all over the love that was actually surrounding her. At the time, she stopped dancing, and she became depressed and just moaned all the time at her husband, who despite that still stood by her. The following statement could be applicable to both her lives:

Cl.: My husband is totally loving and kind. What's more, he offers me a very decent standard of living as well. He is wonderful with the children. I couldn't ask for any more. And yet I feel like I am missing a particular flair, a spark, that amazing charisma.

I had the impression that it was clear to her after this session that she herself was responsible for her own happiness, and no one else. She had grasped so far that she had completely ignored the part she had to play in a fulfilling relationship, and above all that love is somewhat different from she what she had believed up till then.

Manfred B.—Finding Your True Power

Manfred B. was the kind of person who would help every snail across the road. The retired Catholic religious education teacher from St. Gallen in Switzerland had devoted himself exclusively to his spiritual quest for several years. He looked relaxed and cheerful. However, things were quite different in the previous life that first presented itself to him. In it, he was a brutal slave master in ancient Rome. At the end of it, he himself was killed in a dispute.

His spirit guide had another life in readiness for Manfred, a life during the time of the Nazis.

Cl.: (*Surprised and somewhat irritated.*) It's happened again! I believe I've got a similar job again. (*Pause.*) It's a concentration camp. I am a guard.

U.D.: Why has all this been shown to you?

Cl.: That is a good question.

U.D.: This does seem to be demonstrating some kind of theme, don't you think? What do you think it's all about?

Cl.: (*A longer pause.*) It seems to be about power, about strength ... about applying power sensibly.

After his death in this past life, Manfred had the experience of being a soul in conversation with his spirit guide.

Cl.: Now I am feeling an outburst of rage. It is almost tearing me apart!

U.D.: Why?

Cl.: Because of this life. Because of what I did! Not just because of participating in it, but because I was so entertained by the fear that played out in front of me and that some of them prayed for me not to do anything to them!

U.D.: Let it go again. Take a deep breath. And get back in touch with your spirit guide. Ask your guide what it's all for. Why were these lives shown to you?

Cl.: This power! That's the theme here. In both lives I was very strong, very powerful. But I only did evil things with my power, including against my own soul. I wanted to use this strength just for myself, just for my own ego!

U.D.: Is it a question of recognizing how far one can go when one lives without spirituality?

Cl.: (*Starts trembling.*) Yes! I had a great deal of power, but I actually felt like I was always running into a brick wall.

U.D.: How is it for you today?

Cl.: I think I am on the right path. But sometimes ... I mean, here it is completely reversed. I let myself be completely intimidated by certain people … I make myself small, I cower like a dog. Puh! (*Pause.*) I also don't profess openly that I believe in reincarnation.

U.D.: What do you think that could be about?

Cl.: Actually I know that they aren't really strong. (*Bitterly.*) I have already found that out for myself as the guard and the slave master. No genuine power. Nothing that you might ever submit to.

U.D.: What's on the agenda for you now?

Cl.: Today I have a connection with my soul. I think I need to live that much more fully. Stand up for myself and for the path I have taken! I need more courage and strength.

U.D.: What does your spirit guide think?

Cl.: (*Pause.*) The true power is the one that accompanies God.

Achmed E.—Developmental Steps

Everything that sixty-two-year-old Achmed E.—from Wuppertal in Germany—said during our preliminary discussions could be reduced to a common denominator: "I have gotten nothing by waiting in line, and everyone shoves me to the side." His father had abandoned his wife, the client's mother, when she was pregnant. His stepfather then made the boy's life hell, and his mother couldn't find the strength to stand up for him. At the start of his fifties, Achmed tried to make contact with his biological father, but he didn't respond very positively. Achmed hadn't really succeeded in creating his own happy family either: his wife had abandoned him and their young daughter. However, he looked after the girl lovingly and now she was well established in her career as a doctor.

The theme of rejection ran through Achmed's past life. Initially he saw himself in Spain as a little girl named Anna, whose parents had left the village years earlier. They had forgotten to take her with them, or at least this was the reason that the child used to explain it to herself. She grew up with foster parents. At age sixteen, she was involved in a relationship and got pregnant; straight away the man disappeared without a trace. A few years later she left her foster father, who was by then old and dependent and had just become a widower: "He was restricting me too much," said Anna. At that point, the session stopped. The client gave only indistinct responses. I knew that there must have been something important there for Achmed to look at, but nothing emerged. In such situations I ask the spirit world for help. I went within and into close contact with my spirit guide and that of the client. Suddenly the following questions came to me, and they took the conversation forward:

U.D.: Where's your son?

Cl.: He's fine.

U.D.: Where is he?

Cl.: Don't know.

U.D.: You don't know? What happened?

Cl.: Don't know.

U.D.: I don't believe that you don't know. How long ago did he disappear?

Cl.: … He was small.

U.D.: What happened?

Cl.: Don't know … there's nothing coming.

U.D.: Go back a bit, to that place where you know what happened to him. I'll count to three, then you'll be there! One, two, three.

Cl.: Okay … he is four or five. Um, four.

U.D.: Yes. And?

Cl.: Everyone is leaving … all the men. There's a war. He … Yes, he is going with them.

U.D.: What? That's insane! A four-year-old child going to war?

Cl.: (*Pause.*) He was taken away.

U.D.: Why? Please look at what really happened! Is he ill?

Cl.: No, no.

U.D.: An accident?

Cl.: No.

U.D.: (*Slowly.*) Did you have enough of him and give him away?

Cl.: No!

U.D.: So what happened?

Cl.: (*Very haltingly.*) I, I am sitting there and I am waiting … the child, I am giving him away. They are coming …

U.D.: Who is coming?

Cl.: A married couple, from the city … they are taking the child with them.

U.D.: Why have they taken your son?

Cl.: (*Laughs uncertainly and shrugs his shoulders.*) I wanted them to ... because ... I don't have very much. No money or anything.

U.D.: Do they seem nice?

Cl.: They are well dressed. They definitely have enough money.

U.D.: And how does your son react? Does he just go with them?

Cl.: Yes, I told him to.

U.D.: And how's that for you? What are you feeling?

Cl.: ... Don't know ... I think it will be better for him that way ... There was no more I could give him.

U.D.: Hmm. Maybe he really didn't need very much, apart from a mother's love and a small bite to eat. Why didn't you go work?

Cl.: No, I don't work.

U.D.: Why not? You're young.

Cl.: I like to just sit here.

U.D.: Yes, but you don't get much money that way, do you?

Cl.: No.

U.D.: Take an honest look at yourself. What's the matter with you?

Cl.: I don't like working.

U.D.: And this is exactly how it ends up. So you give your son away and that brings in some money. He was a burden to you and you should have just gotten on with it.

Cl.: Yes. (*Quietly.*) Just so lazy!

In the conversation Achmed had with his spirit guide afterward, one thing was made clear to him: it was important to acknowledge that he had done a better job with his life today than he had in the past. Although he'd had to endure a great deal of rejection in his life, he had looked after his child well and also worked hard enough so that there was always enough for both of them. He'd also had to start learning to forgive, as shown by the steps he had taken to reunite with his father, even though for his entire life he hadn't wanted to know him. In the spirit world, he realized that his foster father's soul during his time as Anna was in his mother during his current life.

For him, it was a matter of standing up for his own feelings from now on, but also of discarding the protective shell of his self-pity and recognizing the progress he was making. Almost incredulous, deeply affected, and also with a touch of pride toward the end of the session, Achmed said about his current life, "I ... oh well ... I am actually quite good at this now, aren't I?"

Hubert G.—Addicted to Love

This fifty-three-year-old branch manager in a department store chain from Graz in Austria seemed at first glance to be open and self-assured. However, what had led him to come to me were agonizing self-doubts: he suffered increasingly often from outbreaks of sweating and from red spots on his face and neck, which appeared whenever he had to meet with a person of whom he had high expectations: business partners, customers, and especially women. On the other hand, he often thought himself rather splendid and noble, albeit in an unpleasantly cool and distant manner.

Once in a trance, Hubert G. found himself in Alsace, as Max the shoemaker, in an inn in the fourteenth century. He was slamming a dice cup down on the table with a crash.

Cl.: I will win. I have to!

U.D.: Why is that?

Cl.: (*Forcing the words out with an effort.*) I have already lost everything.

U.D.: What? What have you lost?

Cl.: Everything. I still have the house, but there's nothing in it anymore. Everything's gone: the workshop, furniture, everything. (*Pause.*) The children were crying as I went back to the inn. (*Pause.*) I can't go back to the house again. I have to win!

As Max, my client experienced the powerful pull of a gambling addiction. It cost him his family, in addition to most of his property. He wife really loved him, but he kept on playing and eventually he left his family so that he wouldn't fritter away the roof over their heads as well. When he looked back at this unhappy life as Max, Hubert became very aware of the parallels with all his current problems.

Cl.: Actually love is the most important thing.

U.D.: More important than everything else?

Cl.: Yes.

U.D.: Back then, did you love your wife and children?

Cl.: Yes, of course. But the dice game was more important.

U.D.: How do you feel about gambling today? Is that an issue for you?

Cl.: That's not an issue anymore. Well, yes, it was an issue once, for a short time, but not anymore.

U.D.: Hmm. Have you fallen into the clutches of anything else?

Cl.: Love.

U.D.: Aha. So does that have the same effect today that gambling did back then?

Cl.: Yeah, I think so.

U.D.: Does it make you happy?

Cl.: Hmm, not really. I feel proud when women want me. When … when they love me.

U.D.: Do they love you? Do you love them?

Cl.: Yes … I don't know …

U.D.: Take a look at your spirit guide. What does he think about this?

Cl.: He tells me that conquering women today gives me the rush that I used to get from gambling. It's an addiction. (*Pause.*) But it's love that I am looking for!

U.D.: What's love for you?

Cl.: Hmm. I am still looking. I think that sex is love too. I don't just get into bed with every woman I meet!

U.D.: Is sex the love that you are seeking?

Cl.: This is confusing … The sex just takes hold of me!

U.D.: Okay. And how is it with love for yourself?

Cl.: (*Quickly.*) I love myself. (*Pause.*) I don't know.

U.D.: You said that the woods are important to you. Do you love nature?

Cl.: (*Cheerfully.*) Oh, yes! Yes, I have that. I love nature. I feel so happy there, so relaxed!

U.D.: That has nothing to do with sex, does it?

Cl.: (*Laughing.*) No.

It was becoming clear to Hubert that once again he was only in pursuit of a rush, but that he would never achieve the love that he was seeking in this way. He was starting to notice that the conquests and the sex had nothing to do with love. He was pleased when his spirit guide showed him that his uncertainty was basically something good. It had stopped him from getting completely lost in his addiction. His uncertainty and his inflamed skin had played an important role by reminding him that it wasn't about the game, but about sincere loving feelings instead.

Martina O.—There's No Fear at Home

Martina O. suffered with a latent fear of life for which she saw no basis in her current life and which eventually led her to come to me.

There are some people who already have an idea what their regression is going to be about, although this is not often the case. However, twenty-two-year-old Martina knew that she must have had a deep connection with Judaism. She dreamt about it, was unusually affected by Jewish music, and would basically always return to its culture. And so in our session she found herself back as a Jewish girl—in a concentration camp.

Cl.: There is always someone who's being picked up. But there are still so many of us children.

U.D.: Yes.

Cl.: I am happy every time someone else gets picked up and not me. I know it's mean, but I try to hide behind someone else.

U.D.: Do you know anyone there?

Cl.: I don't care. (*Cries.*) My parents ... they've gone. Must be in heaven.

U.D.: Yes. How old are you?

Cl.: Nine.

U.D.: What next?

Cl.: (*Loud crying.*)

U.D.: Breathe deeply ... Good, like that. Nice and quiet ... Yes. Now go further. What's happening?

Cl.: (*Horror-struck and breathing heavily.*) They have gotten me. I am screaming. I don't understand. They are wearing the star just like me, but they are so horrible.

U.D.: Look at it all as quickly as you can! Then get through it quickly.

Cl.: They are dragging me and some others into a cellar.

U.D.: What does it look like?

Cl.: It's dark (*Pause.*) I'm afraid. Everyone around me is crying, but so quietly. They are whimpering. It's awful. I don't really understand it properly.

U.D.: You mustn't stay there long. Just get through the whole scenario quickly.

Cl.: I am sitting on the floor. A very small girl is slumped over on my lap, not moving … I stroke her head a little bit, but I am really weak too …

U.D.: Go on a bit further. What's happening?

Cl.: All the children are lying there. Dead. My body is next to the little girl's, fallen on top of it.

U.D.: Where are you?

Cl.: Above, on the ceiling. I am getting away from there quickly. (*Pause.*) Oh, here is my mommy! She waited for me.

U.D.: What does she look like? Like your mommy always did?

Cl.: She is light. (*Relieved laughter.*) She is so beautiful.

U.D.: What is she doing?

Cl.: (*Contented sigh.*) She is hugging me. Daddy is there too. It is so … beautiful. So much love!

U.D.: Enjoy it. Feel it really deep inside you.

Cl.: I am happy but at the same time I feel heavy-hearted.

U.D.: Why?

Cl.: People treated us so badly.

U.D.: Yes.

Cl.: Mommy says that's not important anymore. Everything is good here.

U.D.: Breathe in that feeling that everything is good deep inside you.

Cl.: (*Deeply affected.*) I mustn't have fear anymore. I can trust. It's so big … souls, this heaven … everything is shining brightly. Now I feel very light. I am home.

Martina could state, with regard to her life today, that up until now it lacked precisely this fundamental basic trust, which is that the soul is unshakable, even during the cruelest trials that life can throw at you.

Gustav I.—Being a Burden to Others

Seventy-five-year-old Gustav I., from South Tirol in Italy, was visiting me in secret. His wife had to know nothing of the regression, or she would take him for "godless." He was always trying to be a good person and had been trying all his life to fulfill the expectations of others. He would show those closest to him only certain carefully chosen parts of himself. In his previous life he found himself a very poor woman in Central Africa, who was raising eight children on her own and who had to get through life in the face of persecution, threats, and oppression. While looking back over this life, Gustav suddenly became very sad:

Cl.: In my life now I am so afraid of hurting others … of being a burden to others. I am old already and I haven't learned this yet … still haven't.

U.D.: What then exactly?

Cl.: I want to make it right for everyone … I feel horrible, get more and more foreign to myself … and I like all these other people less and less. The strength that this African woman has, that I had then, I need this today.

U.D.: What does this strength feel like? Try to get back into that feeling.

Cl.: (*Pause.*) My own feelings matter! I am looking after the children so they can survive. I won't let anyone tell me otherwise. I have a lot of dignity!

U.D.: Could that not apply in this life now as well?

Cl.: (*Pause.*) Yes. I would be honest then … and authentic. (*Pause.*) Then I would also become happier again and so more pleasant to everybody! (*Chuckles.*) Well, yes, to some people anyway!

Manuela T.—A Truly Good Shepherd

At the age of thirty-three, Manuela T., a seamstress from Berlin, already had a considerable number of relationships behind her, often with older men who were usually married. Consequently, she was starting to long for the security of a functioning family. This was something she hadn't experienced as a child, as her father's moods were erratic and he drank and gambled. Her parents conducted an "open" relationship; they were always having affairs and so paid little attention to their daughter. As a child and then a young person, my client was often alone or felt herself to be an annoyance.

As an adult, Manuela felt driven by an inner restlessness without experiencing deep feelings. Her eyes would only light up when she spoke of her pet parrot, and then she would radiate warmth and joie de vivre. The first thing she called out when she arrived in her past life was, "Oh, how lovely. I feel at home here!" She described an alpine landscape with mountains that were glowing red and lush meadows, and a flock of sheep that were crowding round her. She was a shepherd named Sepp, a contented, quiet man in the mountains near Innsbruck, in around 1900. Suddenly Sepp started to cry softly:

U.D.: What has happened? Take a look around and tell me what has happened.

Cl.: She's gone.

U.D.: Who?

Cl.: My wife.

U.D.: Hmm. How long ago did that happen? When was that?

Cl.: Twenty-five years ago.

U.D.: And why did she go? What happened?

Cl.: I was always with the sheep.

U.D.: Did she feel lonely? Or why else might she have gone?

Cl.: She wanted to experience things. See people.

U.D.: And you? Couldn't you go with her?

Cl.: I wanted to stay with my sheep.

U.D.: How has it been for you without her these twenty-five years?

Cl.: It hasn't been easy. I still miss her.

U.D.: Yes. Was it a good decision, staying here, or have you regretted it in the meantime?

Cl.: No, I am a shepherd. (*With a great deal of warmth.*) This … this is my group, my family … the sheep.

U.D.: And your wife? She is your family too, surely?

Cl.: I believe she never liked sheep like I did. She didn't want to stay poor like this. I was always a shepherd. That's what

I wanted to be. I was a shepherd a long time before I even met my wife.

U.D.: What was she expecting you to do?

Cl.: Sell my sheep and move into town.

U.D.: Ah. How was that for you?

Cl.: (*Angrily.*) There was never a question of that! That wasn't going to happen!

By the time he was eighty, the shepherd had grown weak. He couldn't get around so easily and wasn't able to look after his sheep anymore. He had to give his animals away to someone else.

Cl.: I hope so very much that they are well treated. It causes me a great deal of worry.

U.D.: How are you now?

Cl.: I don't want to go on anymore. It's the end. I'm done with it all. I'm not really there anymore. It's ... it's almost over.

U.D.: Are you ready to go?

Cl.: Yes.

U.D.: And how do you feel about that?

Cl.: Happy ... and tired.

U.D.: Go to the last moment of this life. What's happening?

Cl.: I can see myself lying on the bed from above.

U.D.: Have you died already?

Cl.: I am still breathing a little bit.

U.D.: Hmm. Go further.

Cl.: I am leaving the body. And I am just sort of floating there.

U.D.: How do you feel about your body as it's lying there?

Cl.: That it was the body.

U.D.: Yes. No more important than that?

Cl.: No, no more important. (*Starts crying.*)

U.D.: Why are you crying now?

Cl.: I am looking at the sheep again.

U.D.: Do that. How are they?

Cl.: (*Sighs with relief.*) They are fine. They are all alive. They are grazing on the mountainside.

U.D.: Do you want to say goodbye? Take your time. (*Pause.*) Do they recognize you?

Cl.: I believe they do.

U.D.: How are they reacting?

Cl.: They … It's so lovely. They are looking up at me … all of them. They are showing their thanks.

U.D.: How are they doing that?

Cl.: I just know that they are.

U.D.: How does that feel for you?

Cl.: It's good. (*Smiles happily and contentedly.*)

U.D.: Take this wonderful feeling deep within you, this great love and warmth that connects you.

In looking back with the spirit guide, the shepherd's soul said that it was proud that it stayed with the sheep. Overall, though, it took itself to task quite harshly and thought that it should have taken better care of the shepherd's wife. The spirit guide reassured it and said that it was very satisfied with the soul. It was a matter of the soul learning in its life, as the shepherd had, to do what lay closest to its heart—and it had done that, even if in some respects it had been very painful. Then again, it would not have been happy if it had chosen the other path, because then it would have neglected its chosen task. Reliability, responsibility, care, devotion, and steadfastness—the soul learned all these things as a shepherd in the mountains.

In conclusion, Manuela felt a deep connection with the contentment of this humble and gracious man who she was then as a shepherd. She seemed relaxed and at peace with herself. Her spirit guide reminded her about her parrot. My client seemed deeply moved that this beloved animal appeared before her in the spirit world. The spirit guide stated to her that this parrot would show her the way to go in her life today. If she could love herself just as much as she loved her bird, and could attend to her true needs as she did to his, then her wild searching and desperate restlessness would come to an end.

Bernd P.—From Person to Person

Bernd P. from Vienna came across to me as a sympathetic and caring man in his late thirties. When he spoke of his children, he radiated love and joy. His wife had been diagnosed with cancer two years prior, but her chances of recovery were good. Bernd had changed since the onset of her illness. He suddenly wanted to know more about the deeper connections between life and death. When asked about the challenges he was currently facing, he said that it had been suggested to him where he worked that he should take some courses in teamwork. He couldn't understand, however, how they could find any fault with him. Naturally he could sometimes be a bit rude, "But the numbers that my team delivers are the best in the company," he said.

The regression took Bernd to the north of Germany where he was one of the land-owning aristocracy living in a splendid property around 1690. He was the undisputed ruler of everything and everyone there—something he clearly enjoyed as a nobleman. As Bernd, this was somewhat unpleasant for him. The nobleman thought himself a good and popular ruler. After a drinking session, he fell down some stairs and died immediately. Instead of ascending into the spirit world, his soul was drawn over the cliffs and deep under the sea.

Cl.: The water is foaming and rushing. (*Frightened.*) Whoa! That looks like some kind of octopus ... with lots of heads ... an infinite number of them!

U.D.: What sort of heads?

Cl.: They are looking around quite angrily.

U.D.: Have they done anything to you?

Cl.: Not yet.

U.D.: What happens next?

Cl.: Now I am being drawn toward a woman. She has very long hair. She's not having a good time. She is really suffering.

U.D.: Aha. Who is she?

Cl.: I have no idea who it is. A woman.

U.D.: Go over to her and ask her what she needs.

Cl.: I can't get to her. There are walls all around her. She's imprisoned.

U.D.: So, does that remind you of anything?

Cl.: (*Shocked.*) Of my wife! (*Pause.*) I had her thrown in a dungeon. That was … seven years ago. After that I didn't really think about it anymore.

U.D.: What?! Why?

Cl.: She betrayed me! With a cup bearer! I had him beheaded.

U.D.: Look at her. What do you feel?

Cl.: Hmm. I don't feel angry anymore. (*Pause.*) She says she betrayed me because I had betrayed her as well, many times, and because I was never there for her. She loved the cup bearer.

U.D.: Why did you imprison her when, after all, you had betrayed her too?

Cl.: That was something I just wasn't going to tolerate! It was against everything I stand for. I am a ruler! I really couldn't let that go!

U.D.: Did you love her?

Cl.: No, I don't believe I did. But I liked her. Huh! Now all those evil-looking heads are getting closer again, horrible! It's all … they are all subjects of mine … yelling and screaming at me … Oh no! I imprisoned or killed all of them too. (*Cries out in terror.*) The octopus's tentacles are trying to grab me!

Just after this unpleasant turn of events, the client's soul managed to reach the spirit world. It tried to justify itself in front of the spirit guide by stating that in those days you just had to be tough as a ruler. Soon, however, the soul realized that this was a flimsy excuse. He had taken advantage of his position and the customs of the time to raise himself up. In a sense he had become intoxicated by power: Ruler over Life and Death. Now as a soul he recognized that it should have been an opportunity to use his power for the greater good and for justice.

U.D.: What can you take from this for your current life?

Cl.: Today I am doing all right.

U.D.: You thought that in the past as well.

Cl.: I am going to care about other people!

U.D.: I believe that you will in your private life.

Cl.: (*Angry.*) Yes, professionally, too. I am sure of that and I won't be like I was in the past!

U.D.: What do you mean? How do you think your colleagues might see things?

Cl.: (*Pause.*) Hmm ... Some of my colleagues might also be waiting in the sea for me and have things to yell at me for. (*Hesitantly.*) Yes, that's true, sometimes maybe I could be a bit nicer.

U.D.: What's preventing you from doing that?

Cl.: Pressure! We have got to perform well, have our numbers in the black and stuff.

U.D.: Will that threaten your mission to be nicer?

Cl.: Hmm. Perhaps I should really try and work more collaboratively, more person to person. But I will still remain the boss.

U.D.: Sounds good.

Cl.: (*Laughing.*) So I'd better get myself off to that seminar on teamwork!

U.D.: Does your spirit guide think that too?

Cl.: (*Irritably.*) Hmm. No, he thinks I should already have done that.

Saskia R.—Like Francis of Assisi

I would have described Saskia R. the first time she appeared at my practice as powerful and inquisitive, with an easy laugh. She was fifty-two years old and had a sense of her life as "all right so far," but she couldn't shrug off the feeling that there should have been more to it. As she lapsed into yet more almost nervous joking, I deliberately spoke to her in a particularly quiet and gentle way until she actually noticed what was happening. "Now I understand a little bit. When I have lost contact with my innermost being and feel uncertain, then I try to distract myself from it so that I can escape this nasty feeling," she said.

As a musician in a municipal orchestra in the German state of Thuringia, she was, as she described it, more preoccupied with the financial constraints around working in a cultural field than with the music itself—and that was pretty trying on the nerves. She also offered cello lessons, which were going slowly. She described the atmosphere in her family—Saskia was married and had three sons—as good "as long as I am able to keep hold of all the different threads."

All these things on top of each other led my client to feel a deep dissatisfaction that often manifested as irritability. Saskia felt restricted and imprisoned in her body. By coming to me with her desire to do a regression, she was now ready to figure out what was the matter with her.

What Saskia then experienced was an astonishing and deeply moving past life. She witnessed herself as a Franciscan monk named Franz in Bavaria. For as long as this young man could remember, he had been the personal servant of Prince Albert, who had reigned from a castle there. In about 1582, however, the prince was poisoned by his rival, Ferdinand. He became seriously ill but did not die. While Ferdinand took over, Brother Franz had been forced to accept that the prince had become insane. He ran through the neighborhood like a wild thing and spoke gibberish.

U.D.: What's happening now?

Cl.: We are in a hut in the forest, the prince and I. No one wants to be with him anymore. He must live here in the forest. I am going to stay with him.

U.D.: Why? Has someone given you orders to do this?

Cl.: No, it's my job to do this. Being here for the prince, that's my life. As a young man, I only had to look after his physical well-being. But since I became a monk, I also care for his spiritual well-being. At my ordination, he wanted me to stay with him from that moment on. This is my place and my life is dedicated to that task.

U.D.: What are you living on?

Cl.: People who like him come by sometimes and bring us
things to eat.

U.D.: How is it for you as a young man—you are twenty-
eight now—to be with a mad person?

Cl.: With his body, it's hard sometimes. I must always take
care that he doesn't run away, get lost, or have an accident
in the forest. (*Pause.*) But he gets quieter as the years pass.
It is so beautiful, with his soul. I speak with it. It shows
itself sometimes.

They lived there together for nearly twenty years. When
there was another change in rulership, people remembered the
earlier prince and he was offered a room back at the castle. The
two of them, however, wanted to stay in the forest, where they
were finally able build a proper stone house for themselves on
the site of the old hut. At around seventy years of age, Albert
started preparing himself for death.

Cl.: It is like a death that goes in waves. His soul goes out of
him and then turns back in. Again and again, and then at
one point it doesn't go back into the body anymore. He is
dead. However, the soul stays with me for a time and also
always comes back to visit me. I have learned a lot from
it, above all, that the body—that which is earthly—isn't so
important. It's all about the spiritual. (*Pause.*) I get a lot of
peace from being with Albert's soul.

Franz doesn't leave this place anymore. He simply stays
where he is. For many more years he lives in the forest, fed by
what others bring him or what the forest provides. In his last

years, a young monk from his order visited him increasingly often because he sensed that he could learn a great deal from this old person.

U.D.: What did you do during this whole time? What sort of life was that, when the prince wasn't there any longer and your mission to look after him had fallen away?

Cl.: (*After a pause.*) I was in the forest a great deal. I was at one with the forest. I had conversations with the plants, trees, and animals.

U.D.: How?

Cl.: Through feelings, an interchange, but we are all one.

U.D.: Did you also pray a lot?

Cl.: Not really in the way we learned to as monks. Actually, not using words at all. I have been so close to nature my whole life, and words would only disturb that.

U.D.: Now go forward to when your life as Brother Franz is reaching its end.

Cl.: Now I am experiencing for myself what I had also observed with Albert. The soul keeps inching its way further out. It wants to experience just one last thing. It wants to go into the woods, but my body just can't manage it anymore. So I sit down in front of my house, the soul draws away, the body stays sitting there and then the soul comes back. And one day it simply doesn't do it again. It stays away and Franz is dead.

Looking back at this special life, the soul and the spirit guide appeared to be very satisfied, as the soul had taken some considerable developmental steps as Franz. Saskia had the feeling that she should take the same steps today, but that she was still a long way from accepting life with the same devotion as Franz. In her conversation with her spirit guide, it became clear to her that it was a question of knowing that the spiritual should always come first.

U.D.: Yes, that is an important realization. What could help you to feel and maintain this connection?

Cl.: I am wondering if music could be that. (*Pause.*) But I don't feel anything there.

U.D.: Music is definitely a good way. Not necessarily for you perhaps, but then again I suppose it could be. Just once, feel very deeply within you how that might be.

Cl.: The way that I make music, there is nothing there to feel. I play without soul.

U.D.: Aha. Do you believe that you could bring your soul into it, though?

Cl.: Yes. That does feel good. Music really is my everything. But I have tripped myself up because I always wanted to make it perfect, I think. To be technically perfect. But that on its own is just cold.

I suggested to my client that she should consciously let her wonderful feeling for life as Brother Franz, his deep connection to nature and to the spiritual world, flow into her current awareness. Saskia then imagined how she could make music, be with her family, and live her whole life while in this state of connectedness.

Anna-Lena F.—Fate Is Her Friend

When she came to me, this forty-one-year-old client from Schaan in the Principality of Liechtenstein felt in the greatest of need. She had suffered for several years from a rapidly advancing form of multiple sclerosis. In addition, her husband had left her, taking their two sons with him and making the legal arrangement that she could only see them for one afternoon every two weeks. "I am going to keep fighting," she said, "but soon I will have no energy left and will need help."

The entry into her past life began with a dull thump: a heavy oxcart collided at full speed with a woman and pulled her under its wheels. She lay there motionless. Anna-Lena F. was experiencing life as a farmer on the box seat of a carriage in Bulgaria around the year 1787.

Cl.: My wife! She is dead! She is lying there.

U.D.: Did she go under the wheels of the carriage? What a horrible accident!

Cl.: Yes.

U.D.: What are your feelings about it?

Cl.: (*After a pause.*) It was no accident. I could have prevented it. But I was so angry with her!

U.D.: Why? What happened?

Cl.: All the hard work. Just the two of us … And she couldn't have children and was always angry with me. I wanted another wife. I wanted children, for the farm. I wanted my mistress living with me. I couldn't go on like that.

U.D.: And? What happened?

Cl.: I … I ran her over. Now I am free.

In those days you could not prove that this wasn't an accident. Nevertheless, it was rumored among the people in the village that his wife, who had inherited the farm from her parents, hadn't died by accident. As a result, the husband's mistress distanced herself from him. From then on, the farmer lived alone and began to regret his actions. By the time of his early death, he had come to terms with himself, but he knew all the same that he had given himself a heavy burden of guilt to bear. As a soul, he emphasized to his spirit guide that in his next life he wanted to learn to have more respect for the lives of others and never again to play with fate. "May God's will be done," he said sternly.

For Anna-Lena, the message that this previous life held for her was as follows: it was a matter of accepting things that might happen in desperate circumstances. She was someone who always wanted to control everything. In her weaker form now, she was still in a way like the farmer was then. He thought he had to make all the decisions over life and death so that it would all fit in with his plan. But now, with Anna-Lena's illness and with her family situation, the control she had over her life had been entirely wrested from her. There was only one healthy way ahead for her: to surrender to what was and to how things were—and not by wrangling or perverting justice, but with an open and humble heart, ready to trust her destiny in a deeper sense.

Roman M.—The Higher Will

For a mature soul who is self-aware as a human and is devoted to their spiritual path, it becomes less and less necessary to go through all sorts of dramatic events in their external life or to work through deep inner crises in order to further their development. There are clients who come to me with no specific problem, but who just want to know even more clearly what lies ahead for them to learn, and whether they are fully aware of their life tasks and are implementing them correctly. They wish to enter into an even deeper and more conscious connection with the spirit world.

Roman M., a fifty-eight-year-old journalist and author, is an example of such a person. He had already experienced regression seven times with me and also spent intensive periods in the life between lives. During the time in which I knew him, he changed a great deal. His sense of joy and vitality was steadily increasing.

In one of the sessions, Roman experienced in his past life that he was following a man who was wearing a gold-embroidered robe—a high official in Tibet. He then looked down at himself and saw a brown monk's habit. It turned out that he was a Franciscan monk who in the thirteenth century had spent several years traveling to Tibet to learn and broaden his horizons. After a few years he headed back to his Italian homeland.

U.D.: What were you just doing then as a monk?

Cl.: I am lying there in front of the altar, praying. I am back from Tibet and back in my home city. I am praying so fervently …

U.D.: What's it all about?

Cl.: I believe that I am asking forgiveness for having had deviant thoughts, for having made this trip to Tibet, and for being disloyal to the beliefs of the Catholic Church. So it was some kind of moral lapse.

U.D.: A moral lapse? What, like having an affair? Think about it: Was that it? Was it wrong?

Cl.: I am very unsure of myself. This self-doubt persists. (*Pause.*) No, it wasn't wrong. I learned and saw a lot. I can't shut my eyes and say that it doesn't mean anything.

In old age, this monk, who in the meantime had left his old order and was wandering from place to place, began to pass on his knowledge. He told young monks—those who seemed open and ready for it—about his journey and what he had experienced in the temples of the Tibetans. He became aware that there was much that was good and worthwhile in both religions, and he wanted to combine them. This didn't please some of the clergy; the monk was captured and publicly burned at the stake. Some of his pupils were forced to watch him die while in chains. To him, it wasn't such a big deal, "because my life is near an end anyway and I am happy to have stayed consistent in my views." As a soul, he left his body, even before the burning pyre was lit.

He also went swiftly through the spirit world without having to rely on directions or greetings, only there was a brown shadow that seemed to be doggedly following him. He thought at first that it was a faithful scholar who had died as well, but then he realized that it was his donkey.

Cl.: Yes, it's the donkey I had in the last few difficult years when I was an old man. Perhaps it died of shock or pain and it wanted to stay with me. I am supposed to lead it with me now wherever I go. I have a pretty good idea of what's what so I can float through rapidly. He just hangs on to my coattails and trusts me.

U.D.: Tell me more about the donkey.

Cl.: He was a good friend, a good companion, my only companion really. He was, so to speak, my life companion while I was on the road. Perhaps he will be with me for a bit longer so that I can take care of him. Then he will go off to his own place in heaven, I think.

U.D.: How are you, now, after this life and this death?

Cl.: I feel good because I know what awaits me. I know now that I am going to have a wonderful time again. And I am keen to tell other souls about the life that's just behind me.

U.D.: Are you also with your spirit guide?

Cl.: Yes. (*Laughs.*) He had been ever so slightly hidden and now he is saying something like, "Don't just rush past me." So now I am turning around and I am drifting over to him.

U.D.: In retrospect, how does this life as a monk seem to you?

Cl.: I think it was mostly good, the initial experience I had in Tibet. I stayed there long enough to discover as much as I needed, and I had no fear of entering this very strange-looking temple with the Tibetan monk. The bit in between was not so good, when I was back home and I dealing with such doubts. That moment when I was lying on the floor of the church and pleading for forgiveness, that wasn't so good. I could have been braver then. I only really managed to be brave right at the end of my life when I was an old man. Then I stood up for the truth. That was more important to me than anything else, but I wasted a lot of time. I should have started standing up for the truth much sooner.

U.D.: But perhaps then you would have been executed much sooner?

Cl.: All the same, I still should have been more daring.

U.D.: What does that tell you about your life today?

Cl.: I believe that I should understand that you are never too old for anything. Back then, the old man made the right decision. You can always reconnect with things that you have neglected for a long time but have always really wanted.

U.D.: What should you be doing? What's it all about for you as Roman?

Cl.: I have to learn to understand these connections on my own, without help … I shouldn't rely on others, not depend on others, but keep on pushing myself and seeking.

U.D.: Aha. Is that okay with you?

Cl.: Yes, that works, absolutely. I tend to like to hang around somewhere or wait to see if something happens or if something is presented to me. I was shown by my spirit guide a beautiful landscape, and it always brings to mind my dog from my life today. I think my dog is meant to help me retreat—an excuse for me to become a little bit more of a recluse, at least for a certain amount of time. To wander through the woods. That's what I learn from him. Patience and trust. Because the dog believes steadfastly in all that's good. He never gives up believing in me.

U.D.: Hmm. Sounds very good. It's telling you that you can be like that too.

Cl.: And something else … Don't just think but also feel more. Feeling is the foundation, the spirit guide is telling me.

In order to deepen his initial experience, Roman underwent another regression a few months later in which he was Agba, a woman in Palestine. She belonged to a Bedouin tribe, where women did not have much to say.

Among Agba's children was Miriam, a beautiful and proud girl. Her mother's greatest longing was for Miriam to break free of those strict rules and live in a very different way. Using all her powers of influence, Agba eventually succeeded in getting Miriam married to a rich Roman, with whom she had two children and enjoyed a fabulous life of luxury.

A few years later, however, things were quite different. Roman experienced the arrival of fifty-year-old Agba on an island via a small boat. There on the shore stood her daughter Miriam.

Cl.: It's as if she had … as if she had leprosy … a very disfigured face …

U.D.: Can you see scars or deformities?

Cl.: Deformities, missing … missing parts, but also the … the hands, now coming out the … emerging from her cloak, they are practically just bones … So, yes, she is just like a … just like a skeletal figure.

U.D.: How do you feel? How is it for you?

Cl.: So, it is like wavering between … feeling threatened and feeling compassion …

U.D.: Yes.

Cl.: I am not absolutely clear yet whether she … no, she is no threat. I think this is a leper colony … Everyone here is ill.

Agba moved to the village to live with her daughter from then on and care for her. She felt guilty about what had happened to Miriam. Agba had arranged this marriage, and Miriam's husband had then banished her to this island as soon as she had shown the first symptoms.

Cl.: This is a decisive turning point for me, as it's also clear that I can't … I can't leave this village ever again, now that I have been here just one time.

U.D.: How do you live there in the time that follows?

Cl.: (*Very moved.*) What's fascinating for me is that on this island, Miriam is like … yes, she has become a strong person, and everyone looks up to her and quite openly gives her all the power there, as if she were the queen of this island, of this leper colony.

U.D.: How does she do this?

Cl.: I believe it's because she is very spiritual. She tells the sick people that it's the mission of every single one of them to endure this disease, and that when they are in the life between lives they will discover the reason for this. She shows them that they shouldn't despair, but should accept these things as … as a lesson and even as a special honor. Although many people in the village laughed at

her at the start, she radiates such conviction and power
that she gives courage to a great number of them.

U.D.: Does she give you courage too? How are you feeling,
Agba?

Cl.: (*Longer pause.*) I will also die of leprosy; I am already
quite badly afflicted. But … I admire her so much, my
daughter. She is standing on the beach and she is exuding
an unbelievable power, and now she is black and gold, like
a grid, a pattern of power that radiates divine light. Her
radiance … yes, she is radiating black and gold. She has
accepted her mission.

U.D.: What's your mission?

Cl.: (*Slowly.*) I believe I should have realized how you can
make a mistake when as a mother you think that you
know your child's destiny. You then point this child in a
direction that you think is the correct one, when it was
actually meant to be a completely different one … (*Pause.*)
And I want to discover more about spiritual power.

Even after her death, Miriam acted like a kind of aura, still
perceptible to the villagers as this gold-black energy grid—for
their protection and as a symbol of power and hope. During
a conversation with her spirit guide, Agba's soul recognized
that she had pressured the girl to go in a very worldly direction. As it had been Miriam's desire to live a spiritual life and
to share with others, her illness was simply the only way she
could be guided away from a life of luxury and back to her
actual mission.

U.D.: Why then was she created so beautiful, with this physical beauty, if it was not intended for her to live through
those physical aspects of herself?

Cl.: I think that this Miriam was just such a mature soul,
who had such a radiance … yes, that those for whom
outward beauty was important could then be made aware
of this great spiritual radiance in the same way as her
outward beauty.

Roman today could now keep this life as Agba close at
hand, as a lesson more than anything that he should become
aware of his indirect influence on others. He recognized his
subtle power to manipulate others, which he had already used
as Agba in arranging the marriage of her daughter. Through
his past lives, Roman learned—along with many other things—
to appreciate a feminine and more indirect style of influencing
others. This was quite different from the masculine, direct style
of "banging your fist on the table." For him, this was to be used
not for personal advantage, but in conjunction with his soul as a
tool for the divine higher will in order to bless others.

chapter sixteen

Why Spiritual Regression?

"You go back to an earlier life in order to move forward in your current one." This is how a colleague from the United States aptly described the potential benefits of a spiritual regression. Profound and positive changes can result on many different levels after a regression session. This is clear to me, not least because of the many loving and beautiful pieces of feedback I've received. For example, one client wrote, "The spiritual regression for me was a gift from heaven that has changed my whole life for the better."

In this chapter I want to address once again the areas of life in which we can renew and change ourselves through a regression. Many of these positive changes take place simply because someone has dared to take that defining step to undergo a regression. Change happens on a more definitive level when the person consciously starts to integrate these experiences into their life.

I would like to say a few words about the secondary benefits that people sometimes wish for from a regression session.

There is this romantic notion that when a person is guided into a past life, afterward they can suddenly speak an exotic and maybe even long-extinct language. I have witnessed this sort of thing only on rare occasion, and even then it consisted of only a few scraps of speech.

It's also not the case that a client can end up mastering Portuguese during and even after a regression, when it was the language of the day in a past life in Portugal. During the session, clients continue to speak in what is their present mother tongue, as the communicating aspect of their current consciousness remains in place. Others hope that the skill of being able to play a musical instrument in their past life could still be maintained in this life as a result of a regression. There are possibilities through hypnotic suggestion to activate certain skills from before and to take them back up to a certain level, but certainly not in the sense that one could suddenly play an instrument or speak in a foreign language with any degree of mastery.

Anyway, that's not what it's all about. Reviving such skills might seem useful initially and sound fascinating, but in most cases they don't really have much to do with the direction that your current life should be taking. It would also detract from the main point of the regression, as we want to discover things through the actual process of learning and developing and not simply through reviving outcomes that are already history.

Dissolving Health and Emotional Blockages

Regression can be very effective in dissolving blockages. We have addressed the resolution of burdensome emotions from the past, the relief of symptoms, the healing of illnesses, and a deeper understanding of the causes or of the meaning that lies behind suffering. Sometimes the spirit world will have to provide an additional lesson, a striking symbol, or some good information for a more healthy way of life. People who have already resigned themselves to dying in some cases receive the message that it's actually not time for them to go yet.

A seriously ill woman was told that she should continue living with courage and she would then be able to provide a great deal of comfort to those who are also sick. The woman took this to heart, and for many years things went much better for her than they had before. Others, however, will be confronted with the inevitability of their imminent death. When they reexperience their own existence in the spirit world, in the energy of their soul and accompanied by their spirit guide, the deeper meaning behind living and dying becomes clearer. Then they know deep down that this one death that stands before them is just not as big or as absolute as it had seemed to them before. People get answers to the important question of whether, in the short time that remains to them, there is still something significant for them to achieve.

There are a few rare cases of spontaneous healing. One client experienced a terrible migraine during a session. I thought that we would have to stop, but she most definitely wanted to continue. In the past life she had been led to, she had killed her rival out of greed because he had played a dirty trick on her. She herself was then shot in the head later on. When she transferred to the spirit world, the soul of the man she murdered was already waiting for her. They reconciled, and the migraine went away, never to return.

Another woman had powerful allergies, especially to cat hair. During her session, in which the theme of "exaggerated lines of demarcation" came up, my cat came wandering into the room—an extremely unusual occurrence—and lay down by the woman. She noticed the cat and even said something to it and placed her hand on it—and there seemed to no longer be a problem. From that exact moment on, all her allergies were gone.

To me, it's important that people don't treat illness as some kind of personal failure. Time and again, people come to a session full of guilt because they believe, for as long as they are experiencing symptoms, that they have done something wrong or been a bad person. It is never as simple as that! Sometimes an unhealthy lifestyle really is the main cause of their illness, but very often it's above all a matter of our innermost convictions. If we believe that something is causing us harm and we do it anyway, this is probably going to cause us even more harm. If instead we focus on our health with joy and lightness, then good health will strive to manifest itself. In this sense, an illness can lead you toward a more conscious and holistic way of life.

It can also become clear that someone is not aware that they should treasure their healthy body. Then some affliction will bring them a lesson, particularly one that shows them that they should pay more attention to their life and their physical body.

In our preliminary meeting, one woman complained, "I have such ugly, fat, horrible legs. I am justified in feeling embarrassed by them." In her past life, she was a small boy who was pinned down during a house fire by a falling beam. He had to live the rest of his long life without legs. After this discovery, the woman said, "I will never say another bad word about my legs! I can run, dance, and jump. My legs are perfect!"

Many deeper causes of illness often remain hidden from us. There are many messages that can lie in our sick state. It's not only a question of getting rid of our illness quicker, but also of what we can learn through it, what it stops us from doing, where it's taking us, how we should live with it, and how we can make the best of the situation. An illness always has an effect on the environment of the patient, and it is then a learning opportunity for that person.

Taking Responsibility for One's Life

For many people, the regression changed their attitude toward things in life that had previously bothered them, perhaps concerning their partner or their job. Up until that point they had just complained about it, but then the responsibility was directed right back at them. It was made clear to them that the other person or the firm they work for are not just there to make them happy. They are asked how much they will really give, and how much they will actively do themselves for the person in front of them or for their own well-being. Frankly, they often do shockingly little.

A person can give their best in every place, at any task, in every job, and with every partner or colleague. Even if the current situation is not one you had always dreamt of, it is the one you are going through. It's about mastering the situation as well and as cheerfully as you can. The next steps will then generate themselves. In as much as you can focus on the positive, on what you like, you can put yourself in a good mood and have a pleasant vibrancy about you. Like a magnet, this by itself draws even more that is pleasing into your life. In this way, you can approach your dreams one step at a time, and they will then come true.

If you would like to find out something specific and you truly want that, it is possible to succeed in this—perhaps not in the exact form you envision, but in essence still. It is important, though, to align yourself with your goal fully and precisely through your thoughts, feelings, and actions. Often you first have to let go of a few beliefs that run counter to it, which might stand in the way of fulfillment. For example, if you believe that a good person shouldn't have any money and you would like to be a good person, it will be very difficult for you to earn money or it will bring you no joy and you will run out of it quickly. If a woman believes that men only use women and pay them no attention and abandon them when they feel like it, a harmonious relationship is hardly going to be possible. Even if she manages to get to know a man, she will most likely view him with suspicion. She will project all possible negative things onto him and thus sabotage the relationship. Then she will see the unpleasant outcome as proof that she was sadly right to have had those negative expectations.

The outside world always mirrors our inner beliefs back to us. Much of the time, it's not a question of what is, but of how we evaluate it.

I asked a woman when she was in a trance how she looked in a past life. She began to rave about how beautiful, voluptuous, and strong she was, with enormous breasts, broad hips, and luscious thighs. The person who was lying there in front of me was a lady who wore a size two and had already looked at a yogurt with a stern and critical eye.

During the regression itself, and above all during the review back in the spirit world, clients recognize that you can make something out of every situation and that there are no irrelevant situations or life circumstances. Nothing is for nothing. Even the discovery that, for example, you ended up killing yourself slowly over the years with mountains of food or cigarettes can have the effect of ensuring that something similar probably won't happen again in the lives that follow. A bad experience that you learn something from isn't a bad experience anymore, but is a meaningful learning step.

Dissolving Blockages in Your Spiritual Development

The spiritual development that a regression can either let loose or bring forward will set in once someone experiences the fact that they have been on this earth already, which usually happens in that moment when they find themselves in another existence. The person no longer merely identifies with their current "I" anymore, but instead gains insight into the fascinating complexity of their being.

Naturally, it is also a tremendous step forward in growth and awareness when a person perceives themselves as a soul and feels the presence of their spirit guide. When a person feels that, in the context of the spirit world, something much greater and loftier than earthly life exists, this can release many blockages on the spiritual level. Development of the personality and self-knowledge will be the outcome.

One client of mine viewed her whole life—her environment, the people around her, and even herself—as cold and unfeeling. Inwardly she felt numb, and everything seemed pointless to her. Then there was one major new development after her regression session: the woman started praying again after decades, albeit in a different way. Now it was no longer a question of her asking for things for herself, but of connecting with the divine, feeling this intensely, and letting it shine out from her.

We are so very much more than what we can see and what we can grasp with our senses. Once anyone has uncovered this for themselves, they will quite naturally feel the desire to dig ever deeper into this knowledge.

chapter seventeen

Help from the Spirit World

We human beings often feel alone, abandoned, and over-whelmed by everyday tasks. Those who have gotten to know their spirit guides know that they can communicate with their guide at any time. In every situation it is possible to request and to feel the spirit guide's help, advice, and loving presence. Perhaps this is the greatest gift that comes out of a regression, in the way that I offer it.

It is completely unimportant whether you perceive the spirit guide as a different presence, as its own higher conscious-ness, or as divine light. If we seek ever deeper for the truth, it gradually gets easier to grasp that even this divine authority is not "another" being that is separate from us, but is a part of ourselves, a part of the cosmic whole.

Overcoming the Fear of Death

The fear of death is deeply rooted in us humans and creeps into almost every aspect of life. But those who have reexperienced their death in a previous life and have gone on to experience great happiness and joy afterward will be largely free from this fear.

One client of mine who had a great fear of dying, ever since the time as a child that she had seen a seriously mutilated car accident victim, experienced a gentle, beautiful death in a past life. She said that it was a reassuring and comforting experience. As she was a rather inexperienced soul, a soul that didn't quite feel properly at home on Earth yet, she was made to understand quite plainly in the spirit world, "First you still have a great deal to attend to here on Earth, so do it with joy and with all your power. Only then will it be time to die."

Personal Life Missions and the Meaning of Life

For every person in every life, there isn't always one single life mission. Maybe someone will have one mission at age twenty, then another at thirty-five, and later another at eighty. However, there will be a common thread running through the whole life and quite often even through many lives.

In most cases, it seems neither necessary nor useful to know each respective life mission right from the start. All the steps that we take to reach an understanding of our deeper life goals are important, and we would not take them and would miss many valuable discoveries if we thought from the start that our real life mission perhaps lay elsewhere.

And so, in the regression, you learn very often "only" what the very next step might be. Only gradually, then, does the real life mission start to crystallize.

For some people, the regression brings a confirmation that they are on a good path. One young and lighthearted client, who campaigned actively for animal protection and worked in a nature protection organization, had refused national service. In the past life that presented itself, he was a small child of the aristocracy who was shot during the French Revolution. Back in the spirit world, he spoke as a soul of his wish to work on this earth for peaceful problem solving. After the session, he felt strengthened in his resolve that it really mattered to him in his life today to promote freedom from violence, as well as mutual respect and compassion. He wasn't struggling with anyone, but was speaking up with a dedication and unwavering commitment about what was closest to his heart.

Many people feel that they are meant to be doing something specific, but then they don't find out during the regression what it is or they don't have the strength or courage to put it into action.

The most important signpost to our life mission is this question: "Is what I am thinking, feeling, and doing just now an expression of my love and my joy?" No one has come to this earth to torment themselves throughout their life and definitely not to torment others. If you align yourself in each moment with joy and love for those around you—by taking small steps in all the everyday things around you—you will, consciously or unconsciously, come into contact with your life mission. And fulfilling that will always bring you joy.

What fulfills us as individuals may vary a great deal, but the joy and enthusiasm that rises up from within is common to everyone who is doing what's right for them. Then they feel light and uplifted, full of vitality and strength. Whoever lives in joy won't have to ask about the meaning of life ever again—they are living the answer.

An elderly client said at the end of a session, "The essence of every being, whether a tree, an animal, or a human, is the divine—and that is always joyful love. Love is equality, harmony, respect for all that is—for all other beings, for the earth, for the cosmos, and for one's self."

chapter eighteen

Regression into the Life Between Lives

In addition to my way of carrying out spiritual regressions into past lives described extensively in this book, I would also like to briefly discuss Dr. Michael Newton's method of guiding clients into the life in between—that is, the life that takes place between lives on Earth.

A life between lives spiritual regression should be carried out after a past-life regression. Doing it in this order is important, because in a past life one has experiences in a world similar to the everyday one we know now, and it is not so different and not that unfamiliar. One must first learn to trust this kind of consciousness travel before taking a much greater step: into the life between lives, as a soul.

Up until now I have covered only a very small part of what a regression into the life between lives might have to offer for personal development. We have discussed the life review in the spirit world: the working through of the life just past during the soul's stay in the spirit world, after the person has just died.

However, in a regression into the life between lives, one goes a lot further and a lot deeper into the spirit world. One really experiences intensely one's soul potential, the connection with the divine light, the all-embracing love, and the eternal source of being, which is probably one of the most wonderful and transformative experiences one could have.

The experience of each client is very different. Here the spirit world determines what it will disclose to an individual that is suitable for their life today on Earth and for their next potential development steps. Perhaps the person will meet their soul group and other souls who are especially closely connected to them. It's possible in the framework of this type of session to meet with the souls of certain dead or still living people and even animals. The person can pose direct questions to their spirit guide and get information in return. Or the client can experience how they plan their earthly life and their missions, and they find out what they've been occupied with in the spirit world and what projects they're involved with there. Perhaps they might learn something about the laws of energy and the creation of matter, or journey to the other planets—to name just a few possibilities.

Our individual life on the Earth takes on—through the experience of a spiritual regression into the life between lives—a vast extra dimension that allows us to understand ourselves even better and experience ourselves at a deeper level. It also puts that life into a completely different light. All these things will give us access to more energy, an inner peace, and a joy in life. Much on this earth will then look less serious and tragic to us. At the same time, we will then stand up for our higher vision more mindfully and with more joy, for our own good as well as good of the Earth and all its creatures. And we will know that we are eternal, divine souls that are full of light.

chapter nineteen

My Offer to You

As part of my spiritual regression practice located in the Salzburg Lake District, I currently offer spiritual regressions in individual sessions and workshops mainly in Austria and in the German language. I recommend my workshops on "Spiritual Regressions, Karma Coaching, and Applied Ethics in Everyday Life" as an ideal preparation and also as follow-up for single sessions. These workshops are suitable for the layperson, but also as skill enhancement for regression therapists. Here I teach small groups of participants the practical and theoretical foundations of spiritual regression and guide them through sound practical exercises and group regressions into the childhood and mother's womb of their current life, into past lives, and into the life between lives as an immortal, divine soul. In addition, I offer training classes to become a Certified Past Life Spiritual Regression Practitioner.

If you have questions, you can also send me an e-mail to the address listed on my website. For sessions in other countries, I would be happy to refer you to other therapists of my confidence.

Detailed, up-to-date information on workshops, training courses, and individual sessions offered by me can be found on my bilingual website (German and English):

www.spiritualregression.de

References

Aufhauser, Michael. Gut Aiderbichl. www.gut-aiderbichl.com. English version available.

Demarmels, Ursula. *Karma Coaching: Wege aus der Schicksalsfalle. (Karma Coaching: Escaping the Trap of Fate.)* Allegria, 2015.

———. "The White Goose." Chapter 9 in *Memories of the Afterlife: Life Between Lives Stories of Personal Transformation,* edited by Michael Newton, PhD, with case studies by members of the Newton Institute. Llewellyn, 2009.

Hacker, Dr. Gerhard W., and Ursula Demarmels. *Die neue Dimension der Gesundheit: Ganzheitlicher Schutz vor belastenden Umwelteinflüssen: Ein Ratgeber aus wissenschaftlicher und spiritueller Sicht. (The New Dimension of Health: Holistic Protection from Environmental Influences: A Guide Book from a Scientific and Spiritual Perspective.)* Südwest, 2008. Kindle edition, 2015.

Lessing, Doris. *Shikasta: Recolonised Planet 5*. Vintage, 1981, and Flamingo, 1984. Kindle edition, 2010.

———. *The Sirian Experiments*. Flamingo, 1994. Kindle edition, 2012.

Newton, Michael. *Destiny of Souls: New Case Studies of Life Between Lives*. Llewellyn, 2000.

———. *Journey of Souls: Case Studies of Life Between Lives*. Llewellyn, 1994.

Newton, Michael, ed., with case studies by members of the Newton Institute. *Memories of the Afterlife: Life between Lives Studies of Personal Transformation*. Llewellyn, 2009.

Roman, Sanaya. *Living with Joy: Keys to Personal Power and Spiritual Transformation*. H. J. Kramer, 2011.

———. *Personal Power Through Awareness: A Guidebook for Sensitive People*. H. J. Kramer, 1986.

———. *Spiritual Growth: Being Your Higher Self*. H. J. Kramer, 1988.

To Write to the Author

If you wish to contact the author or would like more information about this book, please write to the author in care of Llewellyn Worldwide Ltd. and we will forward your request. Both the author and publisher appreciate hearing from you and learning of your enjoyment of this book and how it has helped you. Llewellyn Worldwide Ltd. cannot guarantee that every letter written to the author can be answered, but all will be forwarded. Please write to:

Ursula Demarmels
⁒ Llewellyn Worldwide
2143 Wooddale Drive
Woodbury, MN 55125-2989

Please enclose a self-addressed stamped envelope for reply, or $1.00 to cover costs. If outside the U.S.A., enclose an international postal reply coupon.

GET MORE AT LLEWELLYN.COM

Visit us online to browse hundreds of our books and decks, plus sign up to receive our e-newsletters and exclusive online offers.

- • Free tarot readings • Spell-a-Day • Moon phases
- • Recipes, spells, and tips • Blogs • Encyclopedia
- • Author interviews, articles, and upcoming events

GET SOCIAL WITH LLEWELLYN

Find us on Facebook

www.Facebook.com/LlewellynBooks

Follow us on

www.Twitter.com/Llewellynbooks

GET BOOKS AT LLEWELLYN

LLEWELLYN ORDERING INFORMATION

Order online: Visit our website at www.llewellyn.com to select your books and place an order on our secure server.

Order by phone:
- • Call toll free within the U.S. at 1-877-NEW-WRLD (1-877-639-9753)
- • Call toll free within Canada at 1-866-NEW-WRLD (1-866-639-9753)
- • We accept VISA, MasterCard, and American Express

Order by mail:
Send the full price of your order (MN residents add 6.875% sales tax) in U.S. funds, plus postage and handling to: Llewellyn Worldwide, 2143 Wooddale Drive Woodbury, MN 55125-2989

POSTAGE AND HANDLING

STANDARD (U.S. & Canada):
(Please allow 12 business days)
$25.00 and under, add $4.00.
$25.01 and over, FREE SHIPPING.

INTERNATIONAL ORDERS (airmail only):
$16.00 for one book, plus $3.00 for each additional book.

Visit us online for more shipping options. Prices subject to change.

FREE CATALOG!

To order, call 1-877-NEW-WRLD ext. 8236 or visit our website

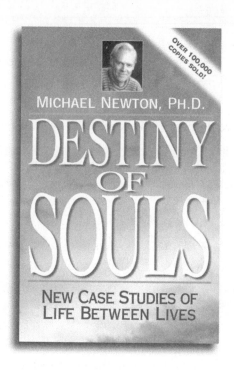

OVER 100,000
COPIES SOLD!

MICHAEL NEWTON, PH.D.

DESTINY
OF
SOULS

NEW CASE STUDIES OF
LIFE BETWEEN LIVES

Destiny of Souls
New Case Studies of Life Between Lives
Michael Newton

Two great spiritual questions many people ponder are as follows: "What existed for me before I was born?" "What will exist for me after my body dies?" You will find the answers to both of these questions in Dr. Michael Newton's book, *Destiny of Souls*.

In this book you will read interviews with sixty-seven people who allowed themselves to be put into a deep state of hypnosis and were regressed to a time between lives. The results will absolutely astound you.

You will discover that between lives there is a place of peace and spiritual education. You'll even find out about recreation and travel between lives. You will discover that there is order and reason in the spirit realms, and what it looks like when you are there. The book reveals the links between soul groups and human families and clearly explains why you chose to incarnate in a certain body.

Answer after answer to your troubling questions will help you experience a lasting peace of heart. Death will no longer be a terrifying end. It will be a transition to even greater peace and love. When you read *Destiny of Souls* you will find yourself happier and more satisfied with life because you will understand who you are and why you are here.

978-1-56718-499-0, 432 pp., 6 x 9   **$17.95**

OVER 250,000
COPIES SOLD!

MICHAEL NEWTON, PH.D.

JOURNEY
OF
SOULS

CASE STUDIES OF
LIFE BETWEEN LIVES

Journey of Souls
Case Studies of Life Between Lives
Michael Newton

Now considered a classic in the field, this remarkable book was the first to fully explore the mystery of life between lives. Journey of Souls presents the first-hand accounts of twenty-nine people placed in a "superconscious" state of awareness using Dr. Michael Newton's groundbreaking techniques. This unique approach allows Dr. Newton to reach his subjects' hidden memories of life in the spirit world after physical death. While in deep hypnosis, the subjects movingly describe what happened to them between lives. They reveal graphic details about what the spirit world is really like, where we go and what we do as souls, and why we come back in certain bodies.

978-1-56718-485-3, 288 pp., 6 x 9   **$16.95**

LIFE
BETWEEN
LIVES

HYPNOTHERAPY
FOR SPIRITUAL REGRESSION

MICHAEL NEWTON
Ph.D.

Life Between Lives
Hypnotherapy for Spiritual Regression
MICHAEL NEWTON

Dr. Michael Newton is world-famous for his spiritual regression techniques that take hypnotic subjects back to their time in the spirit world. His two best-selling books of client case studies, *Journey of Souls* and *Destiny of Souls*, have left thousands of readers eager to discover their own afterlife adventures, their soul companions and guides, and their purpose in this lifetime.

Now, for the first time in print, Dr. Newton reveals his step-by-step methods. His experiential approach to the spiritual realms sheds light on the age-old questions of who we are, where we came from, and why we are here. This groundbreaking guidebook, designed for both hypnosis professionals and the general public, completes the afterlife trilogy by Dr. Newton.

978-0-7387-0465-4, 240 pp., 6 x 9   **$15.95**

MEMORIES
of the
AFTERLIFE

Life Between Lives
Stories of Personal Transformation

Edited by
MICHAEL
NEWTON, PH.D.
with case studies by members of the
NEWTON INSTITUTE

Memories of the Afterlife
Life Between Lives Stories of Personal Transformation
MICHAEL NEWTON

Dr. Michael Newton, best-selling author of *Journey of Souls* and *Destiny of Souls*, returns as the editor and analyst of a series of amazing case studies that highlight the profound impact of spiritual regression on people's everyday lives.

These fascinating true accounts are handpicked and presented by Life Between Lives hypnotherapists certified by the Newton Institute. They feature case studies of real people embarking on life-changing spiritual journeys after recalling their memories of the afterlife: reuniting with soul mates and personal spirit guides, and discovering the ramifications of life and body choices, love relationships, and dreams by communing with their immortal souls. As gems of self-knowledge are revealed, dramatic epiphanies result, enabling these ordinary people to understand adversity in their lives, find emotional healing, realize their true purpose, and forever enrich their lives with new meaning.

978-0-7387-1527-8, 336 pp., 6 x 9   **$17.95**

Past Lives

For Beginners

A Guide to Reincarnation & Techniques
to Improve Your Present Life

DOUGLAS DE LONG

Past Lives for Beginners
A Guide to Reincarnation & Techniques to Improve Your Present Life
Douglas De Long

Explore your previous lifetimes, embrace your wondrous past, and recognize that you, as a human soul, are eternal.

Past Lives for Beginners is a detailed and approachable introduction to understanding reincarnation and how it impacts your present life. Using fascinating case studies, De Long describes different types of past-life recall experiences and shares favored techniques of meditation and visualization used to gain access to those memories. With guidance on how to connect with spirit guides and religious figures, the book also discusses future lives and how to work toward smooth life transitions.

Past Lives for Beginners also includes resources for finding past-life therapists to help you understand your history and forgive past transgressions.

978-0-7387-3517-7, 240 pp., 5³⁄₁₆ x 8   **$13.99**